Visit Cram101.com for full Practice Exams

Visit Cram101.com for full Practice Exams

Textbook Outlines, Highlights, and Practice Quizzes

Family Therapy: Concepts and Methods

by Michael P. Nichols, 10th Edition

All "Just the Facts101" Material Written or Prepared by Cram101 Publishing

Title Page

Visit Cram101.com for full Practice Exams

WHY STOP HERE... THERE'S MORE ONLINE

With technology and experience, we've developed tools that make studying easier and efficient. Like this Cram101 textbook notebook, Cram101.com offers you the highlights from every chapter of your actual textbook. However, unlike this notebook, Cram101.com gives you practice tests for each of the chapters. You also get access to in-depth reference material for writing essays and papers.

By purchasing this book, you get 50% off the normal subscription free!. Just enter the promotional code **'DK73DW20893'** on the Cram101.com registration screen.

CRAMI0I.COM FEATURES:

Outlines & Highlights
Just like the ones in this notebook, but with links to additional information.

Integrated Note Taking
Add your class notes to the Cram101 notes, print them and maximize your study time.

Problem Solving
Step-by-step walk throughs for math, stats and other disciplines.

Practice Exams
Five different test taking formats for every chapter.

Easy Access
Study any of your books, on any computer, anywhere.

Unlimited Textbooks
All the features above for virtually all your textbooks, just add them to your account at no additional cost.

Be sure to use the promo code above when registering on Cram101.com to get 50% off your membership fees.

Visit Cram101.com for full Practice Exams

STUDYING MADE EASY

This Cram101 notebook is designed to make studying easier and increase your comprehension of the textbook material. Instead of starting with a blank notebook and trying to write down everything discussed in class lectures, you can use this Cram101 textbook notebook and annotate your notes along with the lecture.

Our goal is to give you the best tools for success.

For a supreme understanding of the course, pair your notebook with our online tools. Should you decide you prefer Cram101.com as your study tool,

we'd like to offer you a trade...

Our Trade In program is a simple way for us to keep our promise and provide you the best studying tools, regardless of where you purchased your Cram101 textbook notebook. As long as your notebook is in *Like New Condition**, you can send it back to us and we will immediately give you a Cram101.com account free for 120 days!

Let The *Trade In* Begin!

THREE SIMPLE STEPS TO TRADE:

1. Go to www.cram101.com/tradein and fill out the packing slip information.

2. Submit and print the packing slip and mail it in with your Cram101 textbook notebook.

3. Activate your account after you receive your email confirmation.

* Books must be returned in *Like New Condition*, meaning there is no damage to the book including, but not limited to; ripped or torn pages, markings or writing on pages, or folded / creased pages. Upon receiving the book, Cram101 will inspect it and reserves the right to terminate your free Cram101.com account and return your textbook notebook at the owners expense.

Visit Cram101.com for full Practice Exams

"Just the Facts101" is a Cram101 publication and tool designed to give you all the facts from your textbooks. Visit Cram101.com for the full practice test for each of your chapters for virtually any of your textbooks.

Cram101 has built custom study tools specific to your textbook. We provide all of the factual testable information and unlike traditional study guides, we will never send you back to your textbook for more information.

YOU WILL NEVER HAVE TO HIGHLIGHT A BOOK AGAIN!

Cram101 StudyGuides
All of the information in this StudyGuide is written specifically for your textbook. We include the key terms, places, people, and concepts... the information you can expect on your next exam!

Want to take a practice test?
Throughout each chapter of this StudyGuide you will find links to cram101.com where you can select specific chapters to take a complete test on, or you can subscribe and get practice tests for up to 12 of your textbooks, along with other exclusive cram101.com tools like problem solving labs and reference libraries.

Cram101.com
Only cram101.com gives you the outlines, highlights, and PRACTICE TESTS specific to your textbook. Cram101.com is an online application where you'll discover study tools designed to make the most of your limited study time.

By purchasing this book, you get 50% off the normal monthly subscription fee!. Just enter the promotional code **'DK73DW20893'** on the Cram101.com registration screen.

www.Cram101.com

Copyright © 2013 by Cram101, Inc. All rights reserved.
"Just the FACTS101"®, "Cram101"® and "Never Highlight a Book Again!"® are registered trademarks of Cram101, Inc.
ISBN(s): 9781478461975. PUBE-5.2013515

Learning System

Visit Cram101.com for full Practice Exams

Family Therapy: Concepts and Methods
Michael P. Nichols, 10th

CONTENTS

1. The Evolution of Family Therapy 5
2. Basic Techniques of Family Therapy: From Symptom to System 19
3. The Fundamental Concepts of Family Therapy 27
4. Bowen Family Systems Therapy 35
5. Strategic Family Therapy 41
6. Structural Family Therapy 47
7. Experiential Family Therapy 53
8. Psychoanalytic Family Therapy 59
9. Cognitive-Behavioral Family Therapy 67
10. Family Therapy in the Twenty-First Century 77
11. Solution-Focused Therapy 87
12. Narrative Therapy 93
13. Comparative Analysis 99
14. Research on Family Intervention 108

Chapter 1. The Evolution of Family Therapy

CHAPTER OUTLINE: KEY TERMS, PEOPLE, PLACES, CONCEPTS

	Family therapy
	Dysfunctional family
	Psychotherapy
	Self-actualization
	Transference
	Unconditional positive regard
	Group dynamics
	Wilfred Bion
	Alfred Adler
	Group psychotherapy
	Virginia Satir
	John Bowlby
	Tavistock Clinic
	Double bind
	Robin Skynner
	Identified patient
	Theodore Lidz
	Reciprocity
	Paul Popenoe

Visit Cram101.com for full Practice Exams

Chapter 1. The Evolution of Family Therapy
CHAPTER OUTLINE: KEY TERMS, PEOPLE, PLACES, CONCEPTS

- R. D. Laing
- Thought disorder
- Deviance
- Psychodrama
- Brief psychotherapy
- Differentiation
- Mental health
- Loyalty
- Mara Selvini Palazzoli
- Paradox
- Pragmatics
- Psychodynamics
- Structural family therapy

Visit Cram101.com for full Practice Exams

Chapter 1. The Evolution of Family Therapy

CHAPTER HIGHLIGHTS & NOTES: KEY TERMS, PEOPLE, PLACES, CONCEPTS

Family therapy	Family therapy, also referred to as couple and family therapy, family systems therapy, and family counseling, is a branch of psychotherapy that works with families and couples in intimate relationships to nurture change and development. It tends to view change in terms of the systems of interaction between family members. It emphasizes family relationships as an important factor in psychological health.
Dysfunctional family	A dysfunctional family is a family in which conflict, misbehavior, and often child neglect or abuse on the part of individual parents occur continually and regularly, leading other members to accommodate such actions. Children sometimes grow up in such families with the understanding that such an arrangement is normal. Dysfunctional families are primarily a result of co-dependent adults, and may also be affected by addictions, such as substance abuse (alcohol, drugs, etc.)., or sometimes an untreated mental illness.
Psychotherapy	Psychotherapy is a general term referring to therapeutic interaction or treatment contracted between a trained professional and a client, patient, family, couple, or group. The problems addressed are psychological in nature and of no specific kind or degree, but rather depend on the specialty of the practitioner. Psychotherapy aims to increase the individual's sense of his/her own well-being.
Self-actualization	Self-actualization is a term that has been used in various psychology theories, often in slightly different ways. The term was originally introduced by the organismic theorist Kurt Goldstein for the motive to realize one's full potential. In his view, it is the organism's master motive, the only real motive: 'the tendency to actualize itself as fully as possible is the basic drive...the drive of self-actualization.' Carl Rogers similarly wrote of 'the curative force in psychotherapy - man's tendency to actualize himself, to become his potentialities...to express and activate all the capacities of the organism.' However, the concept was brought most fully to prominence in Abraham Maslow's hierarchy of needs theory as the final level of psychological development that can be achieved when all basic and mental needs are fulfilled and the 'actualization' of the full personal potential takes place.
Transference	Transference is a phenomenon in psychoanalysis characterized by unconscious redirection of feelings from one person to another. One definition of transference is 'the inappropriate repetition in the present of a relationship that was important in a person's childhood.' Another definition is 'the redirection of feelings and desires and especially of those unconsciously retained from childhood toward a new object.' Still another definition is 'a reproduction of emotions relating to repressed experiences, esp[ecially] of childhood, and the substitution of another person ... for the original object of the repressed impulses.' Transference was first described by Sigmund Freud, who acknowledged its importance for psychoanalysis for better understanding of the patient's feelings.

Chapter 1. The Evolution of Family Therapy

CHAPTER HIGHLIGHTS & NOTES: KEY TERMS, PEOPLE, PLACES, CONCEPTS

	Occurrence
	It is common for people to transfer feelings from their parents to their partners or children (i.e., cross-generational entanglements).
Unconditional positive regard	Unconditional positive regard, a term popularly believed to have been coined by the humanist Carl Rogers, is basic acceptance and support of a person regardless of what the person says or does. Rogers believes that unconditional positive regard is essential to healthy development. People who have not been exposed to it may come to see themselves in the negative ways that others have made them feel.
Group dynamics	Group dynamics is the study of groups, and also a general term for group processes. Relevant to the fields of psychology, sociology, and communication studies, a group is two or more individuals who are connected to each other by social relationships. Because they interact and influence each other, groups develop a number of dynamic processes that separate them from a random collection of individuals.
Wilfred Bion	Wilfred Ruprecht Bion DSO (8 September 1897 - 8 November 1979) was an influential British psychoanalyst, who became president of the British Psychoanalytical Society from 1962 to 1965.
	Bion has been twinned with Jacques Lacan as 'inspired bizarre analysts...who demand not that their patients get better but that they pursue Truth'. 'Bion's ideas are highly unique', so that he 'remained larger than life to almost all who encountered him'. He has been considered by Neville Symington as possibly 'the greatest psychoanalytic thinker...after Freud'. Military service
	Bion was born in Mathura, North-Western Provinces, India, and educated at Bishop's Stortford College in England. After the outbreak of the First World War, he served in the Tank Corps as a tank commander in France, and was awarded both the Distinguished Service Order (DSO) (on 18 February 1918, for his actions at the Battle of Cambrai), and the Croix de Chevalier of the Légion d'honneur. He first entered the war zone on 26 June 1917, and was promoted to temporary lieutenant on 10 June 1918, and to acting captain on 22 March 1918, when he took command of a tank section, he retained the rank when he became second-in-command of a tank company on 19 October 1918, and relinquished it on 7 January 1919. He was demobilised on 1 September 1921, and was granted the rank of captain. The full citation for his DSO reads:"
	'Bion's daughter, Parthenope ... raises the question of just how (and how far) her father was shaped as an analyst by his wartime experiences...under[p]inning Bion's later concern with the coexistence of regressed or primitive proto-mental states alongside more sophisticated one'. Career

Chapter 1. The Evolution of Family Therapy

CHAPTER HIGHLIGHTS & NOTES: KEY TERMS, PEOPLE, PLACES, CONCEPTS

After World War I, Bion studied history at Queen's College, Oxford and medicine at University College London. Initially attracted to London by the 'strange new subject called psychoanalysis', he met and was impressed by Wilfred Trotter, an outstanding brain surgeon who had also written the famous Instincts of the Herd in Peace and War in 1916, based on the horrors of the First World War. This was to prove an important influence on Bion's interest in group behaviour. Having obtained his medical qualification Bion spent seven years in psychotherapeutic training at the Tavistock Clinic, an experience he regarded, in retrospect, as having had some limitations. It did, however, bring him into fruitful contact with Samuel Beckett. He wanted to train in Psychoanalysis and in 1938 he began a training analysis with John Rickman, but this was brought to an end by the Second World War.

He was recommissioned in the Royal Army Medical Corps as a lieutenant on 1 April 1940, and worked in a number of military hospitals including Northfield Hospital where he initiated the first Northfield Experiment. These ideas on the psychoanalysis of groups were then taken up and developed by others such as S. H. Foulkes, Rickman, Bridger, Main and Patrick De Mare. The entire group at Tavistock had in fact been taken into the army, and were working on new methods of treatment for psychiatric casualties (those suffering post-traumatic stress, or 'shell shock' as it was then known). Out of this his pioneering work in group dynamics, associated with the 'Tavistock group', Bion wrote the influential , London: Tavistock, 1961. Experiences in Groups was an important guide for the group psychotherapy and encounter group movements beginning in the 1960s, and quickly became a touchstone work for applications of group theory in a wide variety of fields.

During the war Bion's wife gave birth to a daughter, but, tragically, she died soon afterwards. His daughter, Parthenope, became a highly-regarded psychoanalyst. She herself died prematurely, in a car crash in Italy in 1998.

Returning to the Tavistock Clinic Bion chaired the Planning Committee that reorganised the Tavistock into the new Tavistock Institute of Human Relations, alongside a new Tavistock Clinic which was part of the newly launched National Health Service. As his interest in psychoanalysis increased, he underwent training analysis, between 1946-1952, with Melanie Klein. He met his second wife, Francesca, at the Tavistock in 1951. He joined a research group of Klein's students (including Hanna Segal and Herbert Rosenfeld), who were developing Klein's theory of the paranoid-schizoid position, for use in the analysis of patients with psychotic disorders, and became a leading member of the Kleinian school. He produced a series of highly original and influential papers (collected as 'Second Thoughts', 1967) on the analysis of schizophrenia, and the specifically cognitive, perceptual, and identity problems of such patients.

Bion's theories, which were always based in the phenomena of the analytic encounter, eventually revealed radical departures from both Kleinian and Freudian theory.

Visit Cram101.com for full Practice Exams

Chapter 1. The Evolution of Family Therapy

CHAPTER HIGHLIGHTS & NOTES: KEY TERMS, PEOPLE, PLACES, CONCEPTS

	At one point, he attempted to understand thoughts and thinking from a mathematical and scientific point of view, believing there to be too little precision in the existing vocabulary, a process culminating in 'The Grid'. Later he abandoned the complex, abstract applications of mathematics, and the Grid, and developed a more intuitive approach, epitomised in the Memoir of the Future.
	He spent his later years in Los Angeles, California, before returning to the UK shortly before his death.
	He left a reputation which has steadily grown both in Britain and internationally. Some commentators consider that his writings are often gnomic and irritating, but never fail to stimulate. He defies categorisation as a follower of Klein or of Freud. While Bion is most well known outside of the psychoanalytic community for his work on group dynamics, the psychoanalytic conversation that explores his work is mainly concerned with his theory of thinking, and his model of the development of a capacity for thought. Group dynamics - the 'basic assumptions'
	Wilfred Bion's observations about the role of group processes in group dynamics are set out in Experiences in Groups where he refers to recurrent emotional states of groups as basic assumptions.
Alfred Adler	Alfred Adler was an Austrian medical doctor, psychotherapist, and founder of the school of individual psychology. His emphasis on the importance of feelings of inferiority - the inferiority complex - is recognized as isolating an element which plays a key role in personality development. Alfred Adler considered human beings as an individual whole, therefore he called his psychology 'Individual Psychology' (Orgler 1976).
Group psychotherapy	Group psychotherapy is a form of psychotherapy in which one or more therapists treat a small group of clients together as a group. The term can legitimately refer to any form of psychotherapy when delivered in a group format, including Cognitive behavioural therapy or Interpersonal therapy, but it is usually applied to psychodynamic group therapy where the group context and group process is explicitly utilised as a mechanism of change by developing, exploring and examining interpersonal relationships within the group. The broader concept of group therapy can be taken to include any helping process that takes place in a group, including support groups, skills training groups (such as anger management, mindfulness, relaxation training or social skills training), and psycho-education groups.
Virginia Satir	Virginia Satir was an American author and psychotherapist, known especially for her approach to family therapy and her work with Systemic Constellations. She is widely regarded as the 'Mother of Family Therapy' Her most well-known books are Conjoint Family Therapy, 1964, Peoplemaking, 1972, and The New Peoplemaking, 1988.

Chapter 1. The Evolution of Family Therapy

CHAPTER HIGHLIGHTS & NOTES: KEY TERMS, PEOPLE, PLACES, CONCEPTS

John Bowlby	Edward John Mostyn 'John' John Bowlby was a British psychologist, psychiatrist and psychoanalyst, notable for his interest in child development and for his pioneering work in attachment theory. Family background
	John Bowlby was born in London to an upper-middle-class family. He was the fourth of six children and was brought up by a nanny in the British fashion of his class at that time.
Tavistock Clinic	The Tavistock Clinic is a psychiatric clinic in London, founded in 1920 by Dr. Hugh Crichton-Miller. Notable people associated with the clinic have included Arthur Hyatt Williams, A. K. Rice, David Campbell, Eric Miller, Eric Trist, Hugh Crichton-Miller, Isabel Menzies Lyth, Jock Sutherland, John Bowlby, John Rawlings Rees, Henry Dicks, John Rickman, Esther Bick, Martha Harris, Michael Balint, Pierre Turquet, Robert H. Gosling, Ros Draper, Rosemary Whiffen, Wilfred Bion, Donald Meltzer, and Herbert Phillipson. Early history
	Though Hugh Crichton-Miller was a psychiatrist who developed psychological treatments for shell-shocked soldiers during and after the First World War, clinical services were always for both children and adults, and in fact the clinic's first patient was a child.
Double bind	A double bind is an emotionally distressing dilemma in communication in which an individual receives two or more conflicting messages, in which one message negates the other. This creates a situation in which a successful response to one message results in a failed response to the other (and vice versa), so that the person will be automatically wrong regardless of response. The double bind occurs when the person cannot confront the inherent dilemma, and therefore cannot resolve it or opt out of the situation.
Robin Skynner	Robin Skynner was a Royal Air Force (RAF) pilot who flew the Mosquito twin-engined bomber, and was also a psychiatric pioneer and innovator in the field of treating mental illness. Trained in Group Analysis and working as a child psychiatrist, and a family therapist, he employed group-analytic principles in that therapeutic modality. He was a gifted teacher and practitioner of psychotherapy with individuals, groups, families, couples and institutions.
Identified patient	Identified patient, is a term used in a clinical setting to describe the person in a dysfunctional family who has been subconsciously selected to act out the family's inner conflicts as a diversion; who is the split-off carrier of the (perhaps transgenerational) family disturbance.
	The term is also used in the context of organizational management, in circumstances where an individual becomes the carrier of a group problem. Origins and characteristics

Chapter 1. The Evolution of Family Therapy

CHAPTER HIGHLIGHTS & NOTES: KEY TERMS, PEOPLE, PLACES, CONCEPTS

	The term emerged from the work of the Bateson Project on family homeostasis, as a way of identifying a largely unconscious pattern of behavior whereby an excess of painful feelings in a family lead to one member being identified as the cause of all the difficulties - a scapegoating of the IP. The identified patient - also called the 'symptom-bearer' or 'presenting problem' - may display unexplainable emotional or physical symptoms, and is often the first person to seek help, perhaps at the request of the family.
Theodore Lidz	Theodore Lidz was an American psychiatrist best known for his articles and books on the causes of schizophrenia and on psychotherapy with schizophrenic patients. An advocate of research into environmental causes of mental illness, Lidz was a notable critic of what he saw as a disproportionate focus on biological psychiatry. Born in New York City and raised on Long Island, Lidz attended Columbia College and the Columbia University College of Physicians and Surgeons.
Reciprocity	The social norm of reciprocity is the expectation that people will respond to each other in similar ways-responding to gifts and kindnesses from others with similar benevolence of their own, and responding to harmful, hurtful acts from others with either indifference or some form of retaliation. Such norms can be crude and mechanical, such as a literal reading of the eye-for-an-eye rule lex talionis, or they can be complex and sophisticated, such as a subtle understanding of how anonymous donations to an international organization can be a form of reciprocity for the receipt of very personal benefits, such as the love of a parent. The norm of reciprocity varies widely in its details from situation to situation, and from society to society.
Paul Popenoe	Paul Popenoe was an American founding practitioner of marriage counseling. In his early years, he worked as an agricultural explorer and as a scholar of heredity, where he played a prominent (and, to some in retrospect, notorious) role in the Eugenics movement of the early twentieth century. Born as Paul Bowman Popenoe in Topeka, Kansas in 1888, he was the son of Marion Bowman Popenoe and Frederick Oliver Popenoe, a pioneer of the avocado industry.
R. D. Laing	R. D. Laing was a Scottish psychiatrist who wrote extensively on mental illness - in particular, the experience of psychosis. R. D.

Chapter 1. The Evolution of Family Therapy

	Laing's views on the causes and treatment of serious mental dysfunction, greatly influenced by existential philosophy, ran counter to the psychiatric orthodoxy of the day by taking the expressed feelings of the individual patient or client as valid descriptions of lived experience rather than simply as symptoms of some separate or underlying disorder. R. D. Laing was associated with the anti-psychiatry movement, although he rejected the label.
Thought disorder	In psychiatry, a thought disorder or formal thought disorder occurs when an individual has serious problems with thinking, feelings, and behavior. The symptoms can include false belief about self or others, paranoia, hearing or seeing non-existent things, disconnected speech or thinking, and feelings that don't match the situation. People affected by a thought disorder may present with incomprehensible thought patterns and/or language, either speech or writing, that is presumed to reflect thinking.
Deviance	Deviance, in a sociological context, describes actions or behaviors that violate social norms, including formally-enacted rules (e.g., crime), as well as informal violations of social norms (e.g., rejecting folkways and mores). It is the purview of sociologists, psychologists, psychiatrists, and criminologists to study how these norms are created, how they change over time and how they are enforced. Deviance as a violation of social norms Norms are rules and expectations by which members of society are conventionally guided.
Psychodrama	Psychodrama is an action method, often used as a psychotherapy, in which clients use spontaneous dramatization, role playing and dramatic self-presentation to investigate and gain insight into their lives. Developed by Jacob L. Moreno, M.D. (1889-1974) psychodrama includes elements of theater, often conducted on a stage where props can be used. By closely recreating real-life situations, and acting them out in the present, clients have the opportunity to evaluate their behavior and more deeply understand a particular situation in their lives.
Brief psychotherapy	Brief psychotherapy is an umbrella term for a variety of approaches to psychotherapy. It differs from other schools of therapy in that it emphasises (1) a focus on a specific problem and (2) direct intervention. In brief therapy, the therapist takes responsibility for working more pro-actively with the client in order to treat clinical and subjective conditions faster.
Differentiation	Differentiation is a term in system theory (found in sociology). From the viewpoint of this theory, the principal feature of modern society is the increased process of system differentiation as a way of dealing with the complexity of its environment. This is accomplished through the creation of subsystems in an effort to copy within a system the difference between it and the environment.
Mental health	Mental health describes a level of psychological well-being, or an absence of a mental disorder.

Chapter 1. The Evolution of Family Therapy

CHAPTER HIGHLIGHTS & NOTES: KEY TERMS, PEOPLE, PLACES, CONCEPTS

	From the perspective of 'positive psychology' or 'holism', mental health may include an individual's ability to enjoy life, and create a balance between life activities and efforts to achieve psychological resilience. Mental health can also be defined as an expression of emotions, and as signifying a successful adaptation to a range of demands.
Loyalty	Loyalty is faithfulness or a devotion to a person, country, group, or cause. (Philosophers disagree as to what things one can be loyal to. Some, as explained in more detail below, argue that one can be loyal to a broad range of things, whilst others argue that it is only possible for loyalty to be to another person and that it is strictly interpersonal).
Mara Selvini Palazzoli	Mara Selvini Palazzoli was an Italian psychiatrist and founder in 1971, with Gianfranco Cecchin, Luigi Boscolo and Giuliana Prata, of the systemic and constructivist approach to family therapy which became known as the Milan systems approach. Worked with families of schizophrenic and anorexic children. With her colleagues, she developed a theraputic model that is based on Gregory Bateson's cybernetics theory.
Paradox	A paradox is a statement or group of statements that leads to a contradiction or a situation which (if true) defies logic or reason, similar to circular reasoning. Typically, however, quoted paradoxical statements do not imply a real contradiction and the puzzling results can be rectified by demonstrating that one or more of the premises themselves are not really true, a play on words, faulty and/or cannot all be true together. But many paradoxes, such as Curry's paradox, do not yet have universally accepted resolutions.
Pragmatics	Pragmatics is a subfield of linguistics which studies the ways in which context contributes to meaning. Pragmatics encompasses speech act theory, conversational implicature, talk in interaction and other approaches to language behavior in philosophy, sociology, and linguistics. It studies how the transmission of meaning depends not only on the linguistic knowledge (e.g. grammar, lexicon etc).
Psychodynamics	Psychodynamics is the theory and systematic study of the psychological forces that underlie human behaviour. It is especially interested in the dynamic relations between conscious motivation and unconscious motivation. Sigmund Freud (1856-1939) developed what he called psychodynamics to describe the processes of the mind as flows of psychological energy (Libido) in an organically complex brain.
Structural family therapy	Structural Family Therapy is a method of psychotherapy developed by Salvador Minuchin which addresses problems in functioning within a family. Structural Family Therapists strive to enter, or 'join', the family system in therapy in order to understand the invisible rules which govern its functioning, map the relationships between family members or between subsets of the family, and ultimately disrupt dysfunctional relationships within the family, causing it to stabilize into healthier patterns.

Chapter 1. The Evolution of Family Therapy

CHAPTER QUIZ: KEY TERMS, PEOPLE, PLACES, CONCEPTS

1. _____ was an Italian psychiatrist and founder in 1971, with Gianfranco Cecchin, Luigi Boscolo and Giuliana Prata, of the systemic and constructivist approach to family therapy which became known as the Milan systems approach. Worked with families of schizophrenic and anorexic children. With her colleagues, she developed a theraputic model that is based on Gregory Bateson's cybernetics theory.

   a. Mara Selvini Palazzoli
   b. Valerie Sinason
   c. Milton Trachtenburg
   d. Frances Tustin

2. _____ was an American author and psychotherapist, known especially for her approach to family therapy and her work with Systemic Constellations. She is widely regarded as the 'Mother of Family Therapy' Her most well-known books are Conjoint Family Therapy, 1964, Peoplemaking, 1972, and The New Peoplemaking, 1988.

   She is also known for creating the _____ Change Process Model, a psychological model developed through clinical studies.

   a. Virginia Satir
   b. Kirk J. Schneider
   c. Erich Schrger
   d. Gary Schwartz

3. A _____ is a family in which conflict, misbehavior, and often child neglect or abuse on the part of individual parents occur continually and regularly, leading other members to accommodate such actions. Children sometimes grow up in such families with the understanding that such an arrangement is normal. _____(ies) are primarily a result of co-dependent adults, and may also be affected by addictions, such as substance abuse (alcohol, drugs, etc)., or sometimes an untreated mental illness.

   a. Familialism
   b. Family
   c. Family Environment Scale
   d. Dysfunctional family

4. _____ is the study of groups, and also a general term for group processes. Relevant to the fields of psychology, sociology, and communication studies, a group is two or more individuals who are connected to each other by social relationships. Because they interact and influence each other, groups develop a number of dynamic processes that separate them from a random collection of individuals.

   a. Poverty
   b. Sonja Bernhardt
   c. Group dynamics
   d. British Psychoanalytic Council

Chapter 1. The Evolution of Family Therapy

CHAPTER QUIZ: KEY TERMS, PEOPLE, PLACES, CONCEPTS

5. _____, also referred to as couple and _____, family systems therapy, and family counseling, is a branch of psychotherapy that works with families and couples in intimate relationships to nurture change and development. It tends to view change in terms of the systems of interaction between family members. It emphasizes family relationships as an important factor in psychological health.

   a. Gestalt therapy
   b. Family therapy
   c. Mental health professional
   d. Mental status examination

Visit Cram101.com for full Practice Exams

Visit Cram101.com for full Practice Exams

ANSWER KEY
Chapter 1. The Evolution of Family Therapy

1. a
2. a
3. d
4. c
5. b

You can take the complete Chapter Practice Test

for Chapter 1. The Evolution of Family Therapy
on all key terms, persons, places, and concepts.

Online 99 Cents

http://www.epub126.12.20893.1.cram101.com/

Use www.Cram101.com for all your study needs

including Cram101's online interactive problem solving labs in

chemistry, statistics, mathematics, and more.

Visit Cram101.com for full Practice Exams

Chapter 2. Basic Techniques of Family Therapy: From Symptom to System

CHAPTER OUTLINE: KEY TERMS, PEOPLE, PLACES, CONCEPTS

_____ Family therapy

_____ Genogram

_____ Adolescence

_____ Alcohol abuse

_____ Child abuse

_____ Domestic violence

_____ Substance abuse

_____ Gender role

_____ Diversity

_____ Ethics

_____ Common couple violence

_____ Systems thinking

_____ Managed care

Chapter 2. Basic Techniques of Family Therapy: From Symptom to System

CHAPTER HIGHLIGHTS & NOTES: KEY TERMS, PEOPLE, PLACES, CONCEPTS

Family therapy	Family therapy, also referred to as couple and family therapy, family systems therapy, and family counseling, is a branch of psychotherapy that works with families and couples in intimate relationships to nurture change and development. It tends to view change in terms of the systems of interaction between family members. It emphasizes family relationships as an important factor in psychological health.
Genogram	A genogram is a pictorial display of a person's family relationships and medical history. It goes beyond a traditional family tree by allowing the user to visualize hereditary patterns and psychological factors that punctuate relationships. It can be used to identify repetitive patterns of behavior and to recognize hereditary tendencies.
Adolescence	Adolescence is a transitional stage of physical and psychological human development generally occurring during the period from puberty to legal adulthood (age of majority). The period of adolescence is most closely associated with the teenage years, although its physical, psychological and cultural expressions can begin earlier and end later. For example, although puberty has been historically associated with the onset of adolescent development, it now typically begins prior to the teenage years and there has been a normative shift of it occurring in preadolescence, particularly in females.
Alcohol abuse	Alcohol abuse, as described in the DSM-IV, is a psychiatric diagnosis describing the recurring use of alcoholic beverages despite its negative consequences. Alcohol abuse is sometimes referred to by the less specific term alcoholism. However, many definitions of alcoholism exist, and only some are compatible with alcohol abuse.
Child abuse	Child abuse is the physical, sexual or emotional mistreatment or neglect of a child or children. In the United States, the Centers for Disease Control and Prevention (CDC) and the Department for Children And Families (DCF) define child maltreatment as any act or series of acts of commission or omission by a parent or other caregiver that results in harm, potential for harm, or threat of harm to a child. Child abuse can occur in a child's home, or in the organizations, schools or communities the child interacts with.
Domestic violence	Domestic violence, spousal abuse, battering, family violence, and intimate partner violence (IPV), is defined as a pattern of abusive behaviors by one partner against another in an intimate relationship such as marriage, dating, family, or cohabitation. Domestic violence, so defined, has many forms, including physical aggression or assault (hitting, kicking, biting, shoving, restraining, slapping, throwing objects), or threats thereof; sexual abuse; emotional abuse; controlling or domineering; intimidation; stalking; passive/covert abuse (e.g., neglect); and economic deprivation.

Chapter 2. Basic Techniques of Family Therapy: From Symptom to System

CHAPTER HIGHLIGHTS & NOTES: KEY TERMS, PEOPLE, PLACES, CONCEPTS

Substance abuse	Substance abuse, is a patterned use of a substance (drug) in which the user consumes the substance in amounts or with methods neither approved nor supervised by medical professionals. Substance abuse/drug abuse is not limited to mood-altering or psycho-active drugs. If an activity is performed using the objects against the rules and policies of the matter (as in steroids for performance enhancement in sports), it is also called substance abuse.
Gender role	A gender role is a set of social and behavioral norms that are generally considered appropriate for either a man or a woman in a social or interpersonal relationship. There are differences of opinion as to which observed differences in behavior and personality between genders are entirely due to innate personality of the person and which are due to cultural or social factors, and are therefore the product of socialization, or to what extent gender differences are due to biological and physiological differences. Gender roles differ according to cultural-historical context, and while most cultures express two genders, some express more.
Diversity	In sociology and political studies, the term diversity is used to describe political entities (neighborhoods, student bodies, etc). with members who have identifiable differences in their cultural backgrounds or lifestyles. The term describes differences in racial or ethnic classifications, age, gender, religion, philosophy, physical abilities, socioeconomic background, sexual orientation, gender identity, intelligence, mental health, physical health, genetic attributes, behavior, attractiveness, or other identifying features.
Ethics	Ethics, is a branch of philosophy that involves systematizing, defending, and recommending concepts of right and wrong conduct. It comes from the Greek word ethos, which means 'character'. Major areas of study in ethics may be divided into 4 operational areas:•Meta-ethics, about the theoretical meaning and reference of moral propositions and how their truth values (if any) may be determined;•Normative ethics, about the practical means of determining a moral course of action;•Descriptive ethics, also known as comparative ethics, is the study of people's beliefs about morality;•Applied ethics, about how moral outcomes can be achieved in specific situations; Defining ethics According to Richard Paul and Linda Elder of the Foundation for Critical Thinking, 'most people confuse ethics with behaving in accordance with social conventions, religious beliefs, and the law', and don't treat ethics as a stand-alone concept.

Chapter 2. Basic Techniques of Family Therapy: From Symptom to System

CHAPTER HIGHLIGHTS & NOTES: KEY TERMS, PEOPLE, PLACES, CONCEPTS

Common couple violence	Common couple violence is a type of domestic violence identified by researcher Michael Johnson as a relationship dynamic 'in which conflict occasionally gets 'out of hand,' leading usually to 'minor' forms of violence, and rarely escalates into serious or life-threatening forms of violence.' Johnson contrasts Common couple violence with 'patriarchal terrorism' (PT), a more unilateral form of domestic violence in which a husband engages in a chronic pattern of serious abuse to control a wife, who does not reciprocate with physical aggression. In Common couple violence, acts of violence by men and women occur at fairly equal rates, with rare occurrences of injury, and are not committed in an attempt to control a partner. It is estimated that approximately 50% of couples experience Common couple violence in their relationships.
Systems thinking	Systems thinking is the process of understanding how things influence one another within a whole. In nature, systems thinking examples include ecosystems in which various elements such as air, water, movement, plants, and animals work together to survive or perish. In organizations, systems consist of people, structures, and processes that work together to make an organization healthy or unhealthy.
Managed care	The term managed care is used in the United States to describe a variety of techniques intended to reduce the cost of providing health benefits and improve the quality of care ('managed care techniques') for organizations that use those techniques or provide them as services to other organizations ('managed care, or to describe systems of financing and delivering health care to enrollees organized around managed care techniques and concepts ('managed care delivery systems'). According to the United States National Library of Medicine, the term 'managed care' encompasses programs:' ...intended to reduce unnecessary health care costs through a variety of mechanisms, including: economic incentives for physicians and patients to select less costly forms of care; programs for reviewing the medical necessity of specific services; increased beneficiary cost sharing; controls on inpatient admissions and lengths of stay; the establishment of cost-sharing incentives for outpatient surgery; selective contracting with health care providers; and the intensive management of high-cost health care cases. The programs may be provided in a variety of settings, such as Health Maintenance Organizations and Preferred Provider Organizations.'

Visit Cram101.com for full Practice Exams

Chapter 2. Basic Techniques of Family Therapy: From Symptom to System

CHAPTER QUIZ: KEY TERMS, PEOPLE, PLACES, CONCEPTS

1. The term _____ is used in the United States to describe a variety of techniques intended to reduce the cost of providing health benefits and improve the quality of care ('_____ techniques') for organizations that use those techniques or provide them as services to other organizations ('_____, or to describe systems of financing and delivering health care to enrollees organized around _____ techniques and concepts ('_____ delivery systems'). According to the United States National Library of Medicine, the term '_____' encompasses programs:'

   ...intended to reduce unnecessary health care costs through a variety of mechanisms, including: economic incentives for physicians and patients to select less costly forms of care; programs for reviewing the medical necessity of specific services; increased beneficiary cost sharing; controls on inpatient admissions and lengths of stay; the establishment of cost-sharing incentives for outpatient surgery; selective contracting with health care providers; and the intensive management of high-cost health care cases. The programs may be provided in a variety of settings, such as Health Maintenance Organizations and Preferred Provider Organizations.'

   a. Cochrane Collaboration
   b. Health care
   c. Managed care
   d. Cyberstalking

2. _____ is a type of domestic violence identified by researcher Michael Johnson as a relationship dynamic 'in which conflict occasionally gets 'out of hand,' leading usually to 'minor' forms of violence, and rarely escalates into serious or life-threatening forms of violence.' Johnson contrasts _____ with 'patriarchal terrorism' (PT), a more unilateral form of domestic violence in which a husband engages in a chronic pattern of serious abuse to control a wife, who does not reciprocate with physical aggression.

   In _____, acts of violence by men and women occur at fairly equal rates, with rare occurrences of injury, and are not committed in an attempt to control a partner. It is estimated that approximately 50% of couples experience _____ in their relationships.

   a. Complex post-traumatic stress disorder
   b. Common couple violence
   c. Cyberbullying
   d. Cyberstalking

3. . _____, is a branch of philosophy that involves systematizing, defending, and recommending concepts of right and wrong conduct. It comes from the Greek word ethos, which means 'character'. Major areas of study in _____ may be divided into 4 operational areas:•Meta-_____, about the theoretical meaning and reference of moral propositions and how their truth values (if any) may be determined;•Normative _____, about the practical means of determining a moral course of action;•Descriptive _____, also known as comparative _____, is the study of people's beliefs about morality;•Applied _____, about how moral outcomes can be achieved in specific situations; Defining _____

   According to Richard Paul and Linda Elder of the Foundation for Critical Thinking, 'most people confuse _____ with behaving in accordance with social conventions, religious beliefs, and the law', and don't treat _____ as a stand-alone concept.

Chapter 2. Basic Techniques of Family Therapy: From Symptom to System

CHAPTER QUIZ: KEY TERMS, PEOPLE, PLACES, CONCEPTS

    a. State Children's Health Insurance Program
    b. Malaysian New Economic Policy
    c. Meritocracy
    d. Ethics

4. A _____ is a pictorial display of a person's family relationships and medical history. It goes beyond a traditional family tree by allowing the user to visualize hereditary patterns and psychological factors that punctuate relationships. It can be used to identify repetitive patterns of behavior and to recognize hereditary tendencies.

    a. Homeodynamic principle
    b. Mental Research Institute
    c. Genogram
    d. Strategic Family Therapy

5. _____, also referred to as couple and _____, family systems therapy, and family counseling, is a branch of psychotherapy that works with families and couples in intimate relationships to nurture change and development. It tends to view change in terms of the systems of interaction between family members. It emphasizes family relationships as an important factor in psychological health.

    a. Gestalt therapy
    b. Justice Resource Institute
    c. Mental health professional
    d. Family therapy

Visit Cram101.com for full Practice Exams

Visit Cram101.com for full Practice Exams

ANSWER KEY
Chapter 2. Basic Techniques of Family Therapy: From Symptom to System

1. c
2. b
3. d
4. c
5. d

You can take the complete Chapter Practice Test

for Chapter 2. Basic Techniques of Family Therapy: From Symptom to System

on all key terms, persons, places, and concepts.

Online 99 Cents

http://www.epub126.12.20893.2.cram101.com/

Use www.Cram101.com for all your study needs

including Cram101's online interactive problem solving labs in

chemistry, statistics, mathematics, and more.

Visit Cram101.com for full Practice Exams

Chapter 3. The Fundamental Concepts of Family Therapy

CHAPTER OUTLINE: KEY TERMS, PEOPLE, PLACES, CONCEPTS

	Feedback
	Systems theory
	Complex adaptive system
	Constructivism
	Paul Watzlawick
	Social constructionism
	Constructionism
	Family therapy
	Attachment theory
	Externalization
	Narrative
	Narrative therapy
	Mary Ainsworth
	John Bowlby
	Harry Harlow
	Gender role
	Michael White

Visit Cram101.com for full Practice Exams

Chapter 3. The Fundamental Concepts of Family Therapy

CHAPTER HIGHLIGHTS & NOTES: KEY TERMS, PEOPLE, PLACES, CONCEPTS

Feedback	Feedback is a process in which information about the past or the present influences the same phenomenon in the present or future. As part of a chain of cause-and-effect that forms a circuit or loop, the event is said to 'feed back' into itself. Ramaprasad (1983) defines feedback generally as 'information about the gap between the actual level and the reference level of a system parameter which is used to alter the gap in some way', emphasising that the information by itself is not feedback unless translated into action.
Systems theory	Systems theory is the interdisciplinary study of systems in general, with the goal of elucidating principles that can be applied to all types of systems at all nesting levels in all fields of research. The term does not yet have a well-established, precise meaning, but systems theory can reasonably be considered a specialization of systems thinking, a generalization of systems science, a systems approach. The term originates from Bertalanffy's general system theory (GST) and is used in later efforts in other fields, such as the action theory of Talcott Parsons and the social systems theory of Niklas Luhmann.
Complex adaptive system	Complex adaptive systems are special cases of complex systems, often defined as a 'complex macroscopic collection' of relatively 'similar and partially connected micro-structures' - formed in order to adapt to the changing environment, and increase its survivability as a macro-structure. They are complex; in that they are dynamic networks of interactions, and their relationships are not aggregations of the individual static entities. They are adaptive; in that the individual and collective behavior mutate and self-organize corresponding to the change-initiating micro-event or collection of events.
Constructivism	Constructivism is a theory of learning and an approach to education that lays emphasis on the ways that people create meaning of the world through a series of individual constructs. Constructs are the different types of filters we choose to place over our realities to change our reality from chaos to order. Von Glasersfeld describes constructivism as 'a theory of knowledge with roots in philosophy, psychology, and cybernetics'.
Paul Watzlawick	Paul Watzlawick was an Austrian-American psychologist and philosopher. A theoretician in communication theory and radical constructivism, he has commented in the fields of family therapy and general psychotherapy. He was one of the most influential figures at the Mental Research Institute and lived and worked in Palo Alto, California, until his death at the age of 85.
Social constructionism	Social constructionism and social constructivism are sociological theories of knowledge that consider how social phenomena or objects of consciousness develop in social contexts. A social construction (also called a social construct) is a concept or practice that is the construct of a particular group.

Chapter 3. The Fundamental Concepts of Family Therapy

CHAPTER HIGHLIGHTS & NOTES: KEY TERMS, PEOPLE, PLACES, CONCEPTS

Constructionism	Constructionist learning is inspired by the constructivist theory that individual learners construct mental models to understand the world around them. However, constructionism holds that learning can happen most effectively when people are also active in making tangible objects in the real world. In this sense, constructionism is connected with experiential learning, and builds on Jean Piaget's epistemological theory of constructivism.
Family therapy	Family therapy, also referred to as couple and family therapy, family systems therapy, and family counseling, is a branch of psychotherapy that works with families and couples in intimate relationships to nurture change and development. It tends to view change in terms of the systems of interaction between family members. It emphasizes family relationships as an important factor in psychological health.
Attachment theory	Attachment theory describes the dynamics of long-term relationships between humans. Its most important tenet is that an infant needs to develop a relationship with at least one primary caregiver for social and emotional development to occur normally. Attachment theory explains how much the parents' relationship with the child influences development.
Externalization	Externalization means to put something outside of its original borders, especially to put a human function outside of the human body. The opposite of externalization is internalization. In a concrete sense, by taking notes, we can externalize the function of memory which normally belongs in the brain.
Narrative	A narrative is a story that is created in a constructive format (as a work of speech, writing, song, film, television, video games, photography or theatre) that describes a sequence of fictional or non-fictional events. Ultimately its origin is found in the Proto-Indo-European root gno-, 'to know'. The word 'story' may be used as a synonym of 'narrative', but can also be used to refer to the sequence of events described in a narrative.
Narrative therapy	Narrative Therapy is a form of psychotherapy using narrative. It was initially developed during the 1970s and 1980s, largely by Australian Michael White and his friend and colleague, David Epston, of New Zealand. Their approach became prevalent in North America with the 1990 publication of their book, Narrative Means to Therapeutic Ends, followed by numerous books and articles about previously unmanageable cases of anorexia nervosa, ADHD, schizophrenia, and many other problems.
Mary Ainsworth	Mary Ainsworth was an American-Canadian developmental psychologist known for her work in early emotional attachment with 'The Strange Situation' as well as her work in the development of Attachment Theory. Life

Chapter 3. The Fundamental Concepts of Family Therapy

CHAPTER HIGHLIGHTS & NOTES: KEY TERMS, PEOPLE, PLACES, CONCEPTS

	Mary Ainsworth was born in Glendale, Ohio in 1913, oldest of three sisters. parents both graduated from Dickinson College.
John Bowlby	Edward John Mostyn 'John' John Bowlby was a British psychologist, psychiatrist and psychoanalyst, notable for his interest in child development and for his pioneering work in attachment theory. Family background
	John Bowlby was born in London to an upper-middle-class family. He was the fourth of six children and was brought up by a nanny in the British fashion of his class at that time.
Harry Harlow	Harry Harlow was an American psychologist best known for his maternal-separation and social isolation experiments on rhesus monkeys, which demonstrated the importance of care-giving and companionship in social and cognitive development. He conducted most of his research at the University of Wisconsin-Madison, where humanistic psychologist Abraham Maslow worked for a time with him.
	Harry Harlow's experiments were controversial; they included rearing infant macaques in isolation chambers for up to 24 months, from which they emerged severely disturbed.
Gender role	A gender role is a set of social and behavioral norms that are generally considered appropriate for either a man or a woman in a social or interpersonal relationship. There are differences of opinion as to which observed differences in behavior and personality between genders are entirely due to innate personality of the person and which are due to cultural or social factors, and are therefore the product of socialization, or to what extent gender differences are due to biological and physiological differences.
	Gender roles differ according to cultural-historical context, and while most cultures express two genders, some express more.
Michael White	Michael White was an Australian social worker and family therapist.

Chapter 3. The Fundamental Concepts of Family Therapy

CHAPTER QUIZ: KEY TERMS, PEOPLE, PLACES, CONCEPTS

1. _____ is a form of psychotherapy using narrative. It was initially developed during the 1970s and 1980s, largely by Australian Michael White and his friend and colleague, David Epston, of New Zealand.

   Their approach became prevalent in North America with the 1990 publication of their book, Narrative Means to Therapeutic Ends, followed by numerous books and articles about previously unmanageable cases of anorexia nervosa, ADHD, schizophrenia, and many other problems.

   a. Narrative therapy
   b. Neuropsychological test
   c. Paced Auditory Serial Addition Test
   d. Person-centered therapy

2. Edward John Mostyn 'John' _____ was a British psychologist, psychiatrist and psychoanalyst, notable for his interest in child development and for his pioneering work in attachment theory. Family background

   _____ was born in London to an upper-middle-class family. He was the fourth of six children and was brought up by a nanny in the British fashion of his class at that time.

   a. Angelo F. Coniglio
   b. John Bowlby
   c. Alyssa Rubino
   d. Association of Business Psychologists

3. _____ is a process in which information about the past or the present influences the same phenomenon in the present or future. As part of a chain of cause-and-effect that forms a circuit or loop, the event is said to 'feed back' into itself.

   Ramaprasad (1983) defines _____ generally as 'information about the gap between the actual level and the reference level of a system parameter which is used to alter the gap in some way', emphasising that the information by itself is not _____ unless translated into action.

   a. State Children's Health Insurance Program
   b. The Kallikak Family
   c. Feedback
   d. The Children of Sanchez

4. . _____ was an Austrian-American psychologist and philosopher. A theoretician in communication theory and radical constructivism, he has commented in the fields of family therapy and general psychotherapy. He was one of the most influential figures at the Mental Research Institute and lived and worked in Palo Alto, California, until his death at the age of 85.

   a. Sonja Bernhardt
   b. Correspondent inference theory
   c. Paul Watzlawick

Visit Cram101.com for full Practice Exams

Chapter 3. The Fundamental Concepts of Family Therapy

CHAPTER QUIZ: KEY TERMS, PEOPLE, PLACES, CONCEPTS

5. A _____ is a story that is created in a constructive format (as a work of speech, writing, song, film, television, video games, photography or theatre) that describes a sequence of fictional or non-fictional events. Ultimately its origin is found in the Proto-Indo-European root gno-, 'to know'.

   The word 'story' may be used as a synonym of '_____', but can also be used to refer to the sequence of events described in a _____.

   a. State Children's Health Insurance Program
   b. Narrative
   c. Bretton Woods system
   d. International adoption

Visit Cram101.com for full Practice Exams

Visit Cram101.com for full Practice Exams

ANSWER KEY
Chapter 3. The Fundamental Concepts of Family Therapy

1. a
2. b
3. c
4. c
5. b

You can take the complete Chapter Practice Test

for Chapter 3. The Fundamental Concepts of Family Therapy
on all key terms, persons, places, and concepts.

Online 99 Cents

http://www.epub126.12.20893.3.cram101.com/

Use www.Cram101.com for all your study needs

including Cram101's online interactive problem solving labs in

chemistry, statistics, mathematics, and more.

Visit Cram101.com for full Practice Exams

Chapter 4. Bowen Family Systems Therapy

CHAPTER OUTLINE: KEY TERMS, PEOPLE, PLACES, CONCEPTS

	Family therapy
	Anxiety
	Pragmatism
	Triangulation
	Alfred Adler
	Frank Sulloway
	Adolescence
	Midlife crisis
	Extended family
	Genogram
	Loyalty
	Countertransference
	Differentiation

Visit Cram101.com for full Practice Exams

Chapter 4. Bowen Family Systems Therapy

CHAPTER HIGHLIGHTS & NOTES: KEY TERMS, PEOPLE, PLACES, CONCEPTS

Family therapy	Family therapy, also referred to as couple and family therapy, family systems therapy, and family counseling, is a branch of psychotherapy that works with families and couples in intimate relationships to nurture change and development. It tends to view change in terms of the systems of interaction between family members. It emphasizes family relationships as an important factor in psychological health.
Anxiety	Anxiety is a psychological and physiological state characterized by somatic, emotional, cognitive, and behavioral components. It is the displeasing feeling of fear and concern. The root meaning of the word anxiety is 'to vex or trouble'; in either presence or absence of psychological stress, anxiety can create feelings of fear, worry, uneasiness, and dread.
Pragmatism	Pragmatism is a philosophical tradition centered on the linking of practice and theory. It describes a process where theory is extracted from practice, and applied back to practice to form what is called intelligent practice. Important positions characteristic of pragmatism include instrumentalism, radical empiricism, verificationism, conceptual relativity, and fallibilism.
Triangulation	Triangulation is most commonly used to express a situation in which one family member will not communicate directly with another family member, but will communicate with a third family member, which can lead to the third family member becoming part of the triangle. The concept originated in the study of dysfunctional family systems, but can describe behaviors in other systems as well, including work. Triangulation can also be used as a label for a form of 'splitting' in which one person plays the third family member against one that he or she is upset about.
Alfred Adler	Alfred Adler was an Austrian medical doctor, psychotherapist, and founder of the school of individual psychology. His emphasis on the importance of feelings of inferiority - the inferiority complex - is recognized as isolating an element which plays a key role in personality development. Alfred Adler considered human beings as an individual whole, therefore he called his psychology 'Individual Psychology' (Orgler 1976).
Frank Sulloway	Frank Sulloway is a visiting Scholar in the Institute of Personality and Social Research at the University of California, Berkeley, and a Visiting Professor in the Department of Psychology. He graduated from Harvard College summa cum laude, and with a Ph.D. in the history of science. He was a visiting scholar at the Massachusetts Institute of Technology.
Adolescence	Adolescence is a transitional stage of physical and psychological human development generally occurring during the period from puberty to legal adulthood (age of majority). The period of adolescence is most closely associated with the teenage years, although its physical, psychological and cultural expressions can begin earlier and end later.

Visit Cram101.com for full Practice Exams

Chapter 4. Bowen Family Systems Therapy

CHAPTER HIGHLIGHTS & NOTES: KEY TERMS, PEOPLE, PLACES, CONCEPTS

Midlife crisis	Midlife crisis is a term coined in 1965 by Elliott Jaques and used in Western societies to describe a period of dramatic self-doubt that is felt by some individuals in the 'middle years' or middle age of life, as a result of sensing the passing of their own youth and the imminence of their old age. Sometimes, a crisis can be triggered by transitions experienced in these years, such as extramarital affairs, andropause or menopause, the death of parents or other causes of grief, unemployment or underemployment, realizing that a job or career is hated but not knowing how else to earn an equivalent living, or children leaving home. The result may be a desire to make significant changes in core aspects of day-to-day life or situation, such as in career, work-life balance, marriage, romantic relationships, big-ticket expenditures, or physical appearance.
Extended family	The term extended family defines that extends beyond the nuclear family consisting of grandparents, aunts, uncles, and cousins all living nearby or in the same household. An example is a married couple lives with either husband or wife's parents. The family changes from nuclear household to extended household.
Genogram	A genogram is a pictorial display of a person's family relationships and medical history. It goes beyond a traditional family tree by allowing the user to visualize hereditary patterns and psychological factors that punctuate relationships. It can be used to identify repetitive patterns of behavior and to recognize hereditary tendencies.
Loyalty	Loyalty is faithfulness or a devotion to a person, country, group, or cause. (Philosophers disagree as to what things one can be loyal to. Some, as explained in more detail below, argue that one can be loyal to a broad range of things, whilst others argue that it is only possible for loyalty to be to another person and that it is strictly interpersonal).
Countertransference	Countertransference is defined as redirection of a psychotherapist's feelings toward a client-or, more generally, as a therapist's emotional entanglement with a client. Early formulations The phenomenon was first defined publicly by Sigmund Freud in 1910 ('The Future Prospects of Psycho-Analytic Therapy') as being 'a result of the patient's influence on [the physician's] unconscious feelings;' although Freud had been aware of it privately for some time, writing to Jung for example in 1909 of the need 'to dominate 'counter-transference', which is after all a permanent problem for us'. Freud stated that since an analyst is a human himself he can easily let his emotions into the client Because Freud saw the countertransference as a purely personal problem for the analyst, he rarely referred to it publicly, and did so almost invariably in terms of a 'warning against any countertransference lying in wait' for the analyst, who 'must recognize this countertransference in himself and master it'.
Differentiation	Differentiation is a term in system theory (found in sociology). From the viewpoint of this theory, the principal feature of modern society is the increased process of system differentiation as a way of dealing with the complexity of its environment.

Chapter 4. Bowen Family Systems Therapy

CHAPTER QUIZ: KEY TERMS, PEOPLE, PLACES, CONCEPTS

1. _____ is a visiting Scholar in the Institute of Personality and Social Research at the University of California, Berkeley, and a Visiting Professor in the Department of Psychology.

    He graduated from Harvard College summa cum laude, and with a Ph.D. in the history of science. He was a visiting scholar at the Massachusetts Institute of Technology.

    a. Francis Sumner
    b. Frank Sulloway
    c. Margot Sunderland
    d. Seiji Takaku

2. A _____ is a pictorial display of a person's family relationships and medical history. It goes beyond a traditional family tree by allowing the user to visualize hereditary patterns and psychological factors that punctuate relationships. It can be used to identify repetitive patterns of behavior and to recognize hereditary tendencies.

    a. Genogram
    b. Mental Research Institute
    c. Relationship education
    d. Strategic Family Therapy

3. _____, also referred to as couple and _____, family systems therapy, and family counseling, is a branch of psychotherapy that works with families and couples in intimate relationships to nurture change and development. It tends to view change in terms of the systems of interaction between family members. It emphasizes family relationships as an important factor in psychological health.

    a. Family therapy
    b. Justice Resource Institute
    c. Mental health professional
    d. Mental status examination

4. _____ is a psychological and physiological state characterized by somatic, emotional, cognitive, and behavioral components. It is the displeasing feeling of fear and concern. The root meaning of the word _____ is 'to vex or trouble'; in either presence or absence of psychological stress, _____ can create feelings of fear, worry, uneasiness, and dread.

    a. Abnormal psychology
    b. Justice Resource Institute
    c. Anxiety
    d. Mental status examination

5. . _____ is a philosophical tradition centered on the linking of practice and theory. It describes a process where theory is extracted from practice, and applied back to practice to form what is called intelligent practice.

Chapter 4. Bowen Family Systems Therapy

CHAPTER QUIZ: KEY TERMS, PEOPLE, PLACES, CONCEPTS

Important positions characteristic of _____ include instrumentalism, radical empiricism, verificationism, conceptual relativity, and fallibilism.

a. State Children's Health Insurance Program
b. Justice Resource Institute
c. Mental health professional
d. Pragmatism

ANSWER KEY
Chapter 4. Bowen Family Systems Therapy

1. b
2. a
3. a
4. c
5. d

You can take the complete Chapter Practice Test

for Chapter 4. Bowen Family Systems Therapy
on all key terms, persons, places, and concepts.

Online 99 Cents

http://www.epub126.12.20893.4.cram101.com/

Use www.Cram101.com for all your study needs

including Cram101's online interactive problem solving labs in

chemistry, statistics, mathematics, and more.

Chapter 5. Strategic Family Therapy

CHAPTER OUTLINE: KEY TERMS, PEOPLE, PLACES, CONCEPTS

	Mental Research Institute
	Family therapy
	Brief psychotherapy
	Milton H. Erickson
	Paul Watzlawick
	Intervention
	Pragmatics
	Feedback
	Reframing
	Neutrality
	Double bind

CHAPTER HIGHLIGHTS & NOTES: KEY TERMS, PEOPLE, PLACES, CONCEPTS

Mental Research Institute	The Palo Alto Mental Research Institute is one of the founding institutions of brief and family therapy. Founded by Don D.
Family therapy	Family therapy, also referred to as couple and family therapy, family systems therapy, and family counseling, is a branch of psychotherapy that works with families and couples in intimate relationships to nurture change and development. It tends to view change in terms of the systems of interaction between family members. It emphasizes family relationships as an important factor in psychological health.
Brief psychotherapy	Brief psychotherapy is an umbrella term for a variety of approaches to psychotherapy.

Visit Cram101.com for full Practice Exams

Chapter 5. Strategic Family Therapy

CHAPTER HIGHLIGHTS & NOTES: KEY TERMS, PEOPLE, PLACES, CONCEPTS

	It differs from other schools of therapy in that it emphasises (1) a focus on a specific problem and (2) direct intervention. In brief therapy, the therapist takes responsibility for working more pro-actively with the client in order to treat clinical and subjective conditions faster.
Milton H. Erickson	Milton H. Erickson, (5 December 1901 in Aurum, Nevada - 25 March 1980 in Phoenix, Arizona) was an American psychiatrist specializing in medical hypnosis and family therapy. He was founding president of the American Society for Clinical Hypnosis and a fellow of the American Psychiatric Association, the American Psychological Association, and the American Psychopathological Association. He is noted for his approach to the unconscious mind as creative and solution-generating.
Paul Watzlawick	Paul Watzlawick was an Austrian-American psychologist and philosopher. A theoretician in communication theory and radical constructivism, he has commented in the fields of family therapy and general psychotherapy. He was one of the most influential figures at the Mental Research Institute and lived and worked in Palo Alto, California, until his death at the age of 85.
Intervention	An intervention is an orchestrated attempt by one or many, people - usually family and friends - to get someone to seek professional help with an addiction or some kind of traumatic event or crisis, or other serious problem. The term intervention is most often used when the traumatic event involves addiction to drugs or other items. Intervention can also refer to the act of using a similar technique within a therapy session.
Pragmatics	Pragmatics is a subfield of linguistics which studies the ways in which context contributes to meaning. Pragmatics encompasses speech act theory, conversational implicature, talk in interaction and other approaches to language behavior in philosophy, sociology, and linguistics. It studies how the transmission of meaning depends not only on the linguistic knowledge (e.g. grammar, lexicon etc).
Feedback	Feedback is a process in which information about the past or the present influences the same phenomenon in the present or future. As part of a chain of cause-and-effect that forms a circuit or loop, the event is said to 'feed back' into itself. Ramaprasad (1983) defines feedback generally as 'information about the gap between the actual level and the reference level of a system parameter which is used to alter the gap in some way', emphasising that the information by itself is not feedback unless translated into action.
Reframing	The term reframing designates a communication technique which has origins in family systems therapy and the work of Virginia Satir. Milton H. Erickson has been associated with reframing and it also forms an important part of Neuro-linguistic programming. In addition, provocative therapy uses reframing with an emphasis on humor.

Chapter 5. Strategic Family Therapy

CHAPTER HIGHLIGHTS & NOTES: KEY TERMS, PEOPLE, PLACES, CONCEPTS

Neutrality	Neutrality is the absence of declared bias. In an argument, a neutral person will not choose a side.
	A neutral country maintains political neutrality, a related but distinct concept.
Double bind	A double bind is an emotionally distressing dilemma in communication in which an individual receives two or more conflicting messages, in which one message negates the other. This creates a situation in which a successful response to one message results in a failed response to the other (and vice versa), so that the person will be automatically wrong regardless of response. The double bind occurs when the person cannot confront the inherent dilemma, and therefore cannot resolve it or opt out of the situation.

CHAPTER QUIZ: KEY TERMS, PEOPLE, PLACES, CONCEPTS

1. The Palo Alto _____ is one of the founding institutions of brief and family therapy. Founded by Don D.

   a. Relationship education
   b. Strategic Family Therapy
   c. Mental Research Institute
   d. Structural family therapy

2. _____, also referred to as couple and _____, family systems therapy, and family counseling, is a branch of psychotherapy that works with families and couples in intimate relationships to nurture change and development. It tends to view change in terms of the systems of interaction between family members. It emphasizes family relationships as an important factor in psychological health.

   a. Gestalt therapy
   b. Justice Resource Institute
   c. Family therapy
   d. Mental status examination

3. . _____, (5 December 1901 in Aurum, Nevada - 25 March 1980 in Phoenix, Arizona) was an American psychiatrist specializing in medical hypnosis and family therapy. He was founding president of the American Society for Clinical Hypnosis and a fellow of the American Psychiatric Association, the American Psychological Association, and the American Psychopathological Association. He is noted for his approach to the unconscious mind as creative and solution-generating.

   a. George Estabrooks
   b. Glenn Harrold

Visit Cram101.com for full Practice Exams

Chapter 5. Strategic Family Therapy

CHAPTER QUIZ: KEY TERMS, PEOPLE, PLACES, CONCEPTS

    c. Ernest Hilgard
    d. Milton H. Erickson

4. _____ was an Austrian-American psychologist and philosopher. A theoretician in communication theory and radical constructivism, he has commented in the fields of family therapy and general psychotherapy. He was one of the most influential figures at the Mental Research Institute and lived and worked in Palo Alto, California, until his death at the age of 85.

    a. Sonja Bernhardt
    b. Glenn Harrold
    c. Ernest Hilgard
    d. Paul Watzlawick

5. The term _____ designates a communication technique which has origins in family systems therapy and the work of Virginia Satir. Milton H. Erickson has been associated with _____ and it also forms an important part of Neuro-linguistic programming. In addition, provocative therapy uses _____ with an emphasis on humor.

    a. Rejection Therapy
    b. Residential treatment center
    c. Response-based therapy
    d. Reframing

Visit Cram101.com for full Practice Exams

ANSWER KEY
Chapter 5. Strategic Family Therapy

1. c
2. c
3. d
4. d
5. d

You can take the complete Chapter Practice Test

for Chapter 5. Strategic Family Therapy
on all key terms, persons, places, and concepts.

Online 99 Cents

http://www.epub126.12.20893.5.cram101.com/

Use www.Cram101.com for all your study needs

including Cram101's online interactive problem solving labs in

chemistry, statistics, mathematics, and more.

Chapter 6. Structural Family Therapy

CHAPTER OUTLINE: KEY TERMS, PEOPLE, PLACES, CONCEPTS

	Family therapy
	Isomorphism
	Criticism
	Scapegoating
	Phobia
	Remarriage
	Empathy
	Competence
	Shaping

CHAPTER HIGHLIGHTS & NOTES: KEY TERMS, PEOPLE, PLACES, CONCEPTS

Family therapy	Family therapy, also referred to as couple and family therapy, family systems therapy, and family counseling, is a branch of psychotherapy that works with families and couples in intimate relationships to nurture change and development. It tends to view change in terms of the systems of interaction between family members. It emphasizes family relationships as an important factor in psychological health.
Isomorphism	In sociology, an isomorphism is a similarity of the processes or structure of one organization to those of another, be it the result of imitation or independent development under similar constraints. There are three main types of isomorphism: normative, coercive and mimetic. The concept of isomorphism was primarily developed by Paul DiMaggio and Walter Powell.

Chapter 6. Structural Family Therapy

CHAPTER HIGHLIGHTS & NOTES: KEY TERMS, PEOPLE, PLACES, CONCEPTS

Criticism	Criticism is the practice of judging the merits and faults of something or someone in an intelligible way:•The judger is called 'the critic'•To engage in criticism is 'to criticize'•One specific item of criticism is called 'a criticism' or a 'critique'
	Criticism can be:•directed toward a person or an animal; at a group, authority or organization; at a specific behaviour; or at an object of some kind (an idea, a relationship, a condition, a process, or a thing)•personal (delivered directly from one person to another, in a personal capacity), or impersonal (expressing the view of an organization, and not aimed at anyone personally)•highly specific and detailed, or very abstract and general•verbal (expressed in language) or non-verbal (expressed symbolically, or expressed through an action or a way of behaving)•explicit (the criticism is clearly stated) or implicit (a criticism is implied by what is being said, but it is not stated openly)•the result of critical thinking or spontaneous impulse
	To criticize does not necessarily imply 'to find fault', but the word is often taken to mean the simple expression of an objection against prejudice, or a disapproval. Often criticism involves active disagreement, but it may only mean 'taking sides'. It could just be an exploration of the different sides of an issue.
Scapegoating	Scapegoating is the practice of singling out any party for unmerited negative treatment or blame as a scapegoat. Scapegoating may be conducted by individuals against individuals (e.g. 'Hattie Francis did it, not me!'), individuals against groups (e.g., 'I failed because our school favors boys'), groups against individuals (e.g., 'Jane was the reason our team didn't win'), and groups against groups (e.g., 'Immigrants are taking all of the jobs').
	A scapegoat may be an adult, sibling, child, employee, peer, ethnic or religious group, or country.
Phobia	A phobia is, when used in the context of clinical psychology, a type of anxiety disorder, usually defined as a persistent fear of an object or situation in which the sufferer commits to great lengths in avoiding, typically disproportional to the actual danger posed, often being recognized as irrational. In the event the phobia cannot be avoided entirely, the sufferer will endure the situation or object with marked distress and significant interference in social or occupational activities.
	The terms distress and impairment as defined by the Diagnostic and Statistical Manual of Mental Disorders, Fourth Edition (DSM-IV-TR) should also take into account the context of the sufferer's environment if attempting a diagnosis.
Remarriage	Remarriage is a marriage that takes place after a previous marital union has ended, as through divorce or widowhood. Some individuals are more likely to remarry than others; the likelihood can differ based on previous relationship status (e.g. divorced vs. widowed), level of interest in establishing a new romantic relationship, gender, race, and age among other factors.

Chapter 6. Structural Family Therapy

CHAPTER HIGHLIGHTS & NOTES: KEY TERMS, PEOPLE, PLACES, CONCEPTS

Empathy	Empathy is the capacity to recognize feelings that are being experienced by another sentient or semi-sentient (in fiction writing) being. Someone may need to have a certain amount of empathy before they are able to feel compassion. The English word was coined in 1909 by Edward B. Titchener as an attempt to translate the German word 'Einfühlungsvermögen', a new phenomenon explored at the end of 19th century mainly by Theodor Lipps.
Competence	In American law, competence concerns the mental capacity of an individual to participate in legal proceedings. Defendants that do not possess sufficient 'competence' are usually excluded from criminal prosecution, while witnesses found not to possess requisite competence cannot testify. The English equivalent is fitness to plead.
Shaping	The differential reinforcement of successive approximations, or more commonly, shaping is a conditioning procedure used primarily in the experimental analysis of behavior. It was introduced by B.F. Skinner with pigeons and extended to dogs, dolphins, humans and other species. In shaping, the form of an existing response is gradually changed across successive trials towards a desired target behavior by rewarding exact segments of behavior.

CHAPTER QUIZ: KEY TERMS, PEOPLE, PLACES, CONCEPTS

1. _____, also referred to as couple and _____, family systems therapy, and family counseling, is a branch of psychotherapy that works with families and couples in intimate relationships to nurture change and development. It tends to view change in terms of the systems of interaction between family members. It emphasizes family relationships as an important factor in psychological health.

   a. Gestalt therapy
   b. Family therapy
   c. Mental health professional
   d. Mental status examination

2. . A _____ is, when used in the context of clinical psychology, a type of anxiety disorder, usually defined as a persistent fear of an object or situation in which the sufferer commits to great lengths in avoiding, typically disproportional to the actual danger posed, often being recognized as irrational. In the event the _____ cannot be avoided entirely, the sufferer will endure the situation or object with marked distress and significant interference in social or occupational activities.

   The terms distress and impairment as defined by the Diagnostic and Statistical Manual of Mental Disorders, Fourth Edition (DSM-IV-TR) should also take into account the context of the sufferer's environment if attempting a diagnosis.

   a. Posttraumatic stress disorder

Chapter 6. Structural Family Therapy

CHAPTER QUIZ: KEY TERMS, PEOPLE, PLACES, CONCEPTS

    b. Primary polydipsia
    c. Pseudologia fantastica
    d. Phobia

3. In sociology, an _____ is a similarity of the processes or structure of one organization to those of another, be it the result of imitation or independent development under similar constraints. There are three main types of _____: normative, coercive and mimetic.

    The concept of _____ was primarily developed by Paul DiMaggio and Walter Powell.

    a. Occupational closure
    b. Isomorphism
    c. Ontological security
    d. Open class system

4. _____ is the practice of judging the merits and faults of something or someone in an intelligible way:•The judger is called 'the critic'•To engage in _____ is 'to criticize'•One specific item of _____ is called 'a _____' or a 'critique'

    _____ can be:•directed toward a person or an animal; at a group, authority or organization; at a specific behaviour; or at an object of some kind (an idea, a relationship, a condition, a process, or a thing)•personal (delivered directly from one person to another, in a personal capacity), or impersonal (expressing the view of an organization, and not aimed at anyone personally)•highly specific and detailed, or very abstract and general•verbal (expressed in language) or non-verbal (expressed symbolically, or expressed through an action or a way of behaving)•explicit (the _____ is clearly stated) or implicit (a _____ is implied by what is being said, but it is not stated openly)•the result of critical thinking or spontaneous impulse

    To criticize does not necessarily imply 'to find fault', but the word is often taken to mean the simple expression of an objection against prejudice, or a disapproval. Often _____ involves active disagreement, but it may only mean 'taking sides'. It could just be an exploration of the different sides of an issue.

    a. Criticism
    b. Psychological subversion
    c. Psychological torture
    d. Psychology of torture

5. . In American law, _____ concerns the mental capacity of an individual to participate in legal proceedings. Defendants that do not possess sufficient '_____' are usually excluded from criminal prosecution, while witnesses found not to possess requisite _____ cannot testify. The English equivalent is fitness to plead.

    a. Competency evaluation
    b. Crime Classification Manual
    c. Competence

Visit Cram101.com for full Practice Exams

Visit Cram101.com for full Practice Exams

ANSWER KEY
Chapter 6. Structural Family Therapy

1. b
2. d
3. b
4. a
5. c

You can take the complete Chapter Practice Test

for Chapter 6. Structural Family Therapy
on all key terms, persons, places, and concepts.

Online 99 Cents

http://www.epub126.12.20893.6.cram101.com/

Use www.Cram101.com for all your study needs

including Cram101's online interactive problem solving labs in

chemistry, statistics, mathematics, and more.

Chapter 7. Experiential Family Therapy

CHAPTER OUTLINE: KEY TERMS, PEOPLE, PLACES, CONCEPTS

- Virginia Satir
- Esalen Institute
- Mental Research Institute
- Attachment theory
- John Bowlby
- Self-actualization
- Gestalt therapy
- Attribution
- Diversity

CHAPTER HIGHLIGHTS & NOTES: KEY TERMS, PEOPLE, PLACES, CONCEPTS

Virginia Satir	Virginia Satir was an American author and psychotherapist, known especially for her approach to family therapy and her work with Systemic Constellations. She is widely regarded as the 'Mother of Family Therapy' Her most well-known books are Conjoint Family Therapy, 1964, Peoplemaking, 1972, and The New Peoplemaking, 1988. She is also known for creating the Virginia Satir Change Process Model, a psychological model developed through clinical studies.
Esalen Institute	The Esalen Institute, commonly just called Esalen, is a residential community and retreat center in Big Sur, California, which focuses upon humanistic alternative education. Esalen is a nonprofit organization devoted to activities such as meditation, massage, Gestalt, yoga, psychology, ecology, and spirituality.

Chapter 7. Experiential Family Therapy

CHAPTER HIGHLIGHTS & NOTES: KEY TERMS, PEOPLE, PLACES, CONCEPTS

Mental Research Institute	The Palo Alto Mental Research Institute is one of the founding institutions of brief and family therapy. Founded by Don D.
Attachment theory	Attachment theory describes the dynamics of long-term relationships between humans. Its most important tenet is that an infant needs to develop a relationship with at least one primary caregiver for social and emotional development to occur normally. Attachment theory explains how much the parents' relationship with the child influences development.
John Bowlby	Edward John Mostyn 'John' John Bowlby was a British psychologist, psychiatrist and psychoanalyst, notable for his interest in child development and for his pioneering work in attachment theory. Family background John Bowlby was born in London to an upper-middle-class family. He was the fourth of six children and was brought up by a nanny in the British fashion of his class at that time.
Self-actualization	Self-actualization is a term that has been used in various psychology theories, often in slightly different ways. The term was originally introduced by the organismic theorist Kurt Goldstein for the motive to realize one's full potential. In his view, it is the organism's master motive, the only real motive: 'the tendency to actualize itself as fully as possible is the basic drive...the drive of self-actualization.' Carl Rogers similarly wrote of 'the curative force in psychotherapy - man's tendency to actualize himself, to become his potentialities...to express and activate all the capacities of the organism.' However, the concept was brought most fully to prominence in Abraham Maslow's hierarchy of needs theory as the final level of psychological development that can be achieved when all basic and mental needs are fulfilled and the 'actualization' of the full personal potential takes place.
Gestalt therapy	Gestalt therapy is an existential/experiential form of psychotherapy that emphasizes personal responsibility, and that focuses upon the individual's experience in the present moment, the therapist-client relationship, the environmental and social contexts of a person's life, and the self-regulating adjustments people make as a result of their overall situation. Gestalt therapy was developed by Fritz Perls, Laura Perls and Paul Goodman in the 1940s and 1950s. Overview Edwin Nevis described Gestalt therapy as 'a conceptual and methodological base from which helping professionals can craft their practice'.
Attribution	Attribution is a concept in social psychology addressing the processes by which individuals explain the causes of behavior and events; attribution theory is an umbrella term for various models that attempt to explain those processes.

Chapter 7. Experiential Family Therapy

CHAPTER HIGHLIGHTS & NOTES: KEY TERMS, PEOPLE, PLACES, CONCEPTS

	Psychological research into attribution began with the work of Fritz Heider in the early part of the 20th century, subsequently developed by others such as Harold Kelley and Bernard Weiner. Background
	Psychological research into attribution began with the work of Fritz Heider during the early years of the 20th century.
Diversity	In sociology and political studies, the term diversity is used to describe political entities (neighborhoods, student bodies, etc). with members who have identifiable differences in their cultural backgrounds or lifestyles.
	The term describes differences in racial or ethnic classifications, age, gender, religion, philosophy, physical abilities, socioeconomic background, sexual orientation, gender identity, intelligence, mental health, physical health, genetic attributes, behavior, attractiveness, or other identifying features.

CHAPTER QUIZ: KEY TERMS, PEOPLE, PLACES, CONCEPTS

1. The Palo Alto _____ is one of the founding institutions of brief and family therapy. Founded by Don D.

   a. Mental Research Institute
   b. Strategic Family Therapy
   c. Brief psychotherapy
   d. Structural family therapy

2. _____ was an American author and psychotherapist, known especially for her approach to family therapy and her work with Systemic Constellations. She is widely regarded as the 'Mother of Family Therapy' Her most well-known books are Conjoint Family Therapy, 1964, Peoplemaking, 1972, and The New Peoplemaking, 1988.

   She is also known for creating the _____ Change Process Model, a psychological model developed through clinical studies.

   a. Helga Schachinger
   b. Virginia Satir
   c. Erich Schrger
   d. Gary Schwartz

3. . The _____, commonly just called Esalen, is a residential community and retreat center in Big Sur, California, which focuses upon humanistic alternative education. Esalen is a nonprofit organization devoted to activities such as meditation, massage, Gestalt, yoga, psychology, ecology, and spirituality.

Chapter 7. Experiential Family Therapy

CHAPTER QUIZ: KEY TERMS, PEOPLE, PLACES, CONCEPTS

The institute offers more than 500 public workshops a year, in addition to conferences, research initiatives, residential work-study programs, and internships.

    a. Est: Playing the Game
    b. Esalen Institute
    c. Family planning
    d. Silvio Fanti

4. _____ describes the dynamics of long-term relationships between humans. Its most important tenet is that an infant needs to develop a relationship with at least one primary caregiver for social and emotional development to occur normally. _____ explains how much the parents' relationship with the child influences development.

    a. Attachment therapy
    b. Attachment theory
    c. Effects of adoption on the birth-mother
    d. International adoption

5. Edward John Mostyn 'John' _____ was a British psychologist, psychiatrist and psychoanalyst, notable for his interest in child development and for his pioneering work in attachment theory. Family background

    _____ was born in London to an upper-middle-class family. He was the fourth of six children and was brought up by a nanny in the British fashion of his class at that time.

    a. Angelo F. Coniglio
    b. John Bowlby
    c. Alyssa Rubino
    d. International adoption

ANSWER KEY
Chapter 7. Experiential Family Therapy

1. a
2. b
3. b
4. b
5. b

You can take the complete Chapter Practice Test

for Chapter 7. Experiential Family Therapy
on all key terms, persons, places, and concepts.

Online 99 Cents

http://www.epub126.12.20893.7.cram101.com/

Use www.Cram101.com for all your study needs

including Cram101's online interactive problem solving labs in

chemistry, statistics, mathematics, and more.

Visit Cram101.com for full Practice Exams

Chapter 8. Psychoanalytic Family Therapy

CHAPTER OUTLINE: KEY TERMS, PEOPLE, PLACES, CONCEPTS

- Family therapy
- John Bowlby
- Narcissism
- Self psychology
- Depression
- Empathy
- Mirroring
- Collusion
- Identification
- Adolescence
- Scapegoating
- Transference
- Dissociation
- Regression
- Loyalty
- Differentiation
- Neutrality
- Countertransference

Visit Cram101.com for full Practice Exams

Chapter 8. Psychoanalytic Family Therapy

CHAPTER HIGHLIGHTS & NOTES: KEY TERMS, PEOPLE, PLACES, CONCEPTS

Family therapy	Family therapy, also referred to as couple and family therapy, family systems therapy, and family counseling, is a branch of psychotherapy that works with families and couples in intimate relationships to nurture change and development. It tends to view change in terms of the systems of interaction between family members. It emphasizes family relationships as an important factor in psychological health.
John Bowlby	Edward John Mostyn 'John' John Bowlby was a British psychologist, psychiatrist and psychoanalyst, notable for his interest in child development and for his pioneering work in attachment theory. Family background John Bowlby was born in London to an upper-middle-class family. He was the fourth of six children and was brought up by a nanny in the British fashion of his class at that time.
Narcissism	Narcissism is a term with a wide range of meanings, depending on whether it is used to describe a central concept of psychoanalytic theory, a mental illness, a social or cultural problem, or simply a personality trait. Except in the sense of primary narcissism or healthy self-love, 'narcissism' usually is used to describe some kind of problem in a person or group's relationships with self and others. In everyday speech, 'narcissism' often means egotism, vanity, conceit, or simple selfishness.
Self psychology	Self psychology is a school of psychoanalytic theory and therapy created by Heinz Kohut and developed in the United States at the Chicago Institute for Psychoanalysis. Self psychology explains psychopathology as being the result of disrupted or unmet developmental needs. Essential to understanding self psychology are the concepts of empathy, self-object, mirroring, idealising, alter ego/twinship and the tripolar self.
Depression	Depression is a state of low mood and aversion to activity that can affect a person's thoughts, behavior, feelings and physical well-being. Depressed people may feel sad, anxious, empty, hopeless, helpless, worthless, guilty, irritable, or restless. They may lose interest in activities that once were pleasurable; experience loss of appetite or overeating, have problems concentrating, remembering details, or making decisions; and may contemplate or attempt suicide.
Empathy	Empathy is the capacity to recognize feelings that are being experienced by another sentient or semi-sentient (in fiction writing) being. Someone may need to have a certain amount of empathy before they are able to feel compassion. The English word was coined in 1909 by Edward B. Titchener as an attempt to translate the German word 'Einfühlungsvermögen', a new phenomenon explored at the end of 19th century mainly by Theodor Lipps.
Mirroring	Mirroring is the behaviour in which one person copies another person usually while in social interaction with them.

Chapter 8. Psychoanalytic Family Therapy

CHAPTER HIGHLIGHTS & NOTES: KEY TERMS, PEOPLE, PLACES, CONCEPTS

	It may include miming gestures, movements, body language, muscle tensions, expressions, tones, eye movements, breathing, tempo, accent, attitude, choice of words or metaphors, and other aspects of communication. It is often observed among couples or close friends.
Collusion	Collusion is an agreement between two or more persons, sometimes illegal and therefore secretive, to limit open competition by deceiving, misleading, or defrauding others of their legal rights, or to obtain an objective forbidden by law typically by defrauding or gaining an unfair advantage. It is an agreement among firms to divide the market, set prices, or limit production. It can involve 'wage fixing, kickbacks, or misrepresenting the independence of the relationship between the colluding parties'.
Identification	Identification is a psychological process whereby the subject assimilates an aspect, property, or attribute of the other and is transformed, wholly or partially, after the model the other provides. It is by means of a series of identifications that the personality is constituted and specified. The roots of the concept can be found in Freud's writings.
Adolescence	Adolescence is a transitional stage of physical and psychological human development generally occurring during the period from puberty to legal adulthood (age of majority). The period of adolescence is most closely associated with the teenage years, although its physical, psychological and cultural expressions can begin earlier and end later. For example, although puberty has been historically associated with the onset of adolescent development, it now typically begins prior to the teenage years and there has been a normative shift of it occurring in preadolescence, particularly in females .
Scapegoating	Scapegoating is the practice of singling out any party for unmerited negative treatment or blame as a scapegoat. Scapegoating may be conducted by individuals against individuals (e.g. 'Hattie Francis did it, not me!'), individuals against groups (e.g., 'I failed because our school favors boys'), groups against individuals (e.g., 'Jane was the reason our team didn't win'), and groups against groups (e.g., 'Immigrants are taking all of the jobs'). A scapegoat may be an adult, sibling, child, employee, peer, ethnic or religious group, or country.
Transference	Transference is a phenomenon in psychoanalysis characterized by unconscious redirection of feelings from one person to another. One definition of transference is 'the inappropriate repetition in the present of a relationship that was important in a person's childhood.' Another definition is 'the redirection of feelings and desires and especially of those unconsciously retained from childhood toward a new object.' Still another definition is 'a reproduction of emotions relating to repressed experiences, esp[ecially] of childhood, and the substitution of another person ... for the original object of the repressed impulses.' Transference was first described by Sigmund Freud, who acknowledged its importance for psychoanalysis for better understanding of the patient's feelings.

Chapter 8. Psychoanalytic Family Therapy

CHAPTER HIGHLIGHTS & NOTES: KEY TERMS, PEOPLE, PLACES, CONCEPTS

	Occurrence
	It is common for people to transfer feelings from their parents to their partners or children (i.e., cross-generational entanglements).
Dissociation	Dissociation is a term in psychology describing a wide array of experiences from mild detachment from immediate surroundings to more severe detachment from physical and emotional reality. It is commonly displayed on a continuum. The major characteristic of all dissociative phenomena involves a detachment from reality - rather than a loss of reality as in psychosis.
Regression	Regression in medicine is a characteristic of diseases to show lighter symptoms without completely disappearing. At a later point, symptoms may return. These symptoms are then called recidive.
Loyalty	Loyalty is faithfulness or a devotion to a person, country, group, or cause. (Philosophers disagree as to what things one can be loyal to. Some, as explained in more detail below, argue that one can be loyal to a broad range of things, whilst others argue that it is only possible for loyalty to be to another person and that it is strictly interpersonal).
Differentiation	Differentiation is a term in system theory (found in sociology). From the viewpoint of this theory, the principal feature of modern society is the increased process of system differentiation as a way of dealing with the complexity of its environment. This is accomplished through the creation of subsystems in an effort to copy within a system the difference between it and the environment.
Neutrality	Neutrality is the absence of declared bias. In an argument, a neutral person will not choose a side. A neutral country maintains political neutrality, a related but distinct concept.
Countertransference	Countertransference is defined as redirection of a psychotherapist's feelings toward a client-or, more generally, as a therapist's emotional entanglement with a client. Early formulations The phenomenon was first defined publicly by Sigmund Freud in 1910 ('The Future Prospects of Psycho-Analytic Therapy') as being 'a result of the patient's influence on [the physician's] unconscious feelings;' although Freud had been aware of it privately for some time, writing to Jung for example in 1909 of the need 'to dominate 'counter-transference', which is after all a permanent problem for us'.

Chapter 8. Psychoanalytic Family Therapy

CHAPTER QUIZ: KEY TERMS, PEOPLE, PLACES, CONCEPTS

1. _____ in medicine is a characteristic of diseases to show lighter symptoms without completely disappearing. At a later point, symptoms may return. These symptoms are then called recidive.

    a. Relative risk
    b. Regression
    c. Reverse epidemiology
    d. Risk factor

2. _____ is a phenomenon in psychoanalysis characterized by unconscious redirection of feelings from one person to another. One definition of _____ is 'the inappropriate repetition in the present of a relationship that was important in a person's childhood.' Another definition is 'the redirection of feelings and desires and especially of those unconsciously retained from childhood toward a new object.' Still another definition is 'a reproduction of emotions relating to repressed experiences, esp[ecially] of childhood, and the substitution of another person ... for the original object of the repressed impulses.' _____ was first described by Sigmund Freud, who acknowledged its importance for psychoanalysis for better understanding of the patient's feelings.

    Occurrence

    It is common for people to transfer feelings from their parents to their partners or children (i.e., cross-generational entanglements).

    a. True self and false self
    b. Transference
    c. Berlin Psychoanalytic Institute
    d. British Psychoanalytic Council

3. _____ is a term with a wide range of meanings, depending on whether it is used to describe a central concept of psychoanalytic theory, a mental illness, a social or cultural problem, or simply a personality trait. Except in the sense of primary _____ or healthy self-love, '_____' usually is used to describe some kind of problem in a person or group's relationships with self and others. In everyday speech, '_____' often means egotism, vanity, conceit, or simple selfishness.

    a. Medical practice
    b. Narcissism
    c. Medical simulation
    d. Medicine chest

4. . _____, also referred to as couple and _____, family systems therapy, and family counseling, is a branch of psychotherapy that works with families and couples in intimate relationships to nurture change and development. It tends to view change in terms of the systems of interaction between family members. It emphasizes family relationships as an important factor in psychological health.

    a. Family therapy

Chapter 8. Psychoanalytic Family Therapy

CHAPTER QUIZ: KEY TERMS, PEOPLE, PLACES, CONCEPTS

    b. Justice Resource Institute
    c. Mental health professional
    d. Mental status examination

5. _____ is a psychological process whereby the subject assimilates an aspect, property, or attribute of the other and is transformed, wholly or partially, after the model the other provides. It is by means of a series of _____s that the personality is constituted and specified. The roots of the concept can be found in Freud's writings.

    a. Identification
    b. Object relations theory
    c. Ontogeny
    d. Unsaid

Visit Cram101.com for full Practice Exams

ANSWER KEY
Chapter 8. Psychoanalytic Family Therapy

1. b
2. b
3. b
4. a
5. a

You can take the complete Chapter Practice Test

for Chapter 8. Psychoanalytic Family Therapy
on all key terms, persons, places, and concepts.

Online 99 Cents

http://www.epub126.12.20893.8.cram101.com/

Use www.Cram101.com for all your study needs

including Cram101's online interactive problem solving labs in

chemistry, statistics, mathematics, and more.

Chapter 9. Cognitive-Behavioral Family Therapy

CHAPTER OUTLINE: KEY TERMS, PEOPLE, PLACES, CONCEPTS

- B. F. Skinner
- Desensitization
- Operant conditioning
- Systematic desensitization
- Functional analysis
- Aaron Temkin Beck
- Reinforcement
- Mediation
- Reciprocity
- Schema
- Arbitrary inference
- Cognitive distortion
- Personalization
- Selective abstraction
- Abstraction
- Contingency management
- Shaping
- Token economy
- Time-out

Chapter 9. Cognitive-Behavioral Family Therapy

CHAPTER OUTLINE: KEY TERMS, PEOPLE, PLACES, CONCEPTS

	Attachment theory
	Assertiveness
	Sexual dysfunction
	Arousal
	Teasing
	Parent Management Training
	Social learning
	Social learning theory

CHAPTER HIGHLIGHTS & NOTES: KEY TERMS, PEOPLE, PLACES, CONCEPTS

B. F. Skinner	Burrhus Frederic 'B. F.' B. F. Skinner was an American psychologist, behaviorist, author, inventor, and social philosopher. He was the Edgar Pierce Professor of Psychology at Harvard University from 1958 until his retirement in 1974. B. F. Skinner invented the operant conditioning chamber, also known as the B. F. Skinner Box.
Desensitization	In psychology, desensitization is defined as the diminished emotional responsiveness to a negative or aversive stimulus after repeated exposure to it. It also occurs when an emotional response is repeatedly evoked in situations in which the action tendency that is associated with the emotion proves irrelevant or unnecessary. Desensitization is a process primarily used to assist individuals unlearn phobias and anxieties and was developed by psychologist Mary Cover Jones.
Operant conditioning	Operant conditioning is a form of learning in which an individual's behavior is modified by its consequences; the behaviour may change in form, frequency, or strength.

Visit Cram101.com for full Practice Exams

Chapter 9. Cognitive-Behavioral Family Therapy

CHAPTER HIGHLIGHTS & NOTES: KEY TERMS, PEOPLE, PLACES, CONCEPTS

	Operant conditioning is a term that was coined by B.F Skinner in 1937 Operant conditioning is distinguished from classical conditioning in that operant conditioning deals with the modification of 'voluntary behaviour' or operant behaviour. Operant behavior operates on the environment and is maintained by its consequences, while classical conditioning deals with the conditioning of reflexive (reflex) behaviours which are elicited by antecedent conditions.
Systematic desensitization	Systematic desensitization is a type of behavioral therapy used in the field of psychology to help effectively overcome phobias and other anxiety disorders. More specifically, it is a type of Pavlovian therapy / classical conditioning therapy developed by a South African psychiatrist, Joseph Wolpe. To begin the process of systematic desensitization, one must first be taught relaxation skills in order to extinguish fear and anxiety responses to specific phobias.
Functional analysis	Functional analysis in behavioral psychology is the application of the laws of operant conditioning to establish the relationships between stimuli and responses. To establish the function of a behavior, one typically examines the 'four-term contingency': first by identifying the Motivating Operations (EO or AO), then identifying the antecedent or trigger of the behavior, identifying the behavior itself as it has been operationalized, and identifying the consequence of the behavior which continues to maintain it. Functional analysis in behavior analysis employs principles derived from the natural science of behavior analysis to determine the 'reason', purpose or motivation for a behavior.
Aaron Temkin Beck	Aaron Temkin Beck is an American psychiatrist and a professor emeritus in the department of psychiatry at the University of Pennsylvania. He is widely regarded as the father of cognitive therapy, and his pioneering theories are widely used in the treatment of clinical depression. Beck also developed self-report measures of depression and anxiety including Beck Depression Inventory (BDI), Beck Hopelessness Scale, Beck Scale for Suicidal Ideation (BSS), Beck Anxiety Inventory (BAI), and Beck Youth Inventories.
Reinforcement	Reinforcement is a term in operant conditioning and behavior analysis for the process of increasing the rate or probability of a behavior (e.g. pulling a lever more frequently) by the delivery or emergence of a stimulus (e.g. a candy) immediately or shortly after the behavior, called a 'response,' is performed. The response strength is assessed by measuring frequency, duration, latency, accuracy, and/or persistence of the response after reinforcement stops. Experimental behavior analysts measured the rate of responses as a primary demonstration of learning and performance in non-humans (e.g. the number of times a pigeon pecks a key in a 10-minute session).
Mediation	Mediation, as used in law, is a form of alternative dispute resolution (ADR), a way of resolving disputes between two or more parties with concrete effects.

Visit Cram101.com for full Practice Exams

Chapter 9. Cognitive-Behavioral Family Therapy

CHAPTER HIGHLIGHTS & NOTES: KEY TERMS, PEOPLE, PLACES, CONCEPTS

	Typically, a third party, the mediator, assists the parties to negotiate a settlement. Disputants may mediate disputes in a variety of domains, such as commercial, legal, diplomatic, workplace, community and family matters.
Reciprocity	The social norm of reciprocity is the expectation that people will respond to each other in similar ways-responding to gifts and kindnesses from others with similar benevolence of their own, and responding to harmful, hurtful acts from others with either indifference or some form of retaliation. Such norms can be crude and mechanical, such as a literal reading of the eye-for-an-eye rule lex talionis, or they can be complex and sophisticated, such as a subtle understanding of how anonymous donations to an international organization can be a form of reciprocity for the receipt of very personal benefits, such as the love of a parent. The norm of reciprocity varies widely in its details from situation to situation, and from society to society.
Schema	A schema, in psychology and cognitive science, describes an organized pattern of thought or behavior. It can also be described as a mental structure of pre-conceived ideas, a framework representing some aspect of the world, or a system of organizing and perceiving new information. Schemata influence attention and the absorption of new knowledge: people are more likely to notice things that fit into their schema, while re-interpreting contradictions to the schema as exceptions or distorting them to fit.
Arbitrary inference	In clinical psychology, arbitrary inference is a type of cognitive bias in which a person quickly draws a conclusion without the requisite evidence. It commonly appears in Aaron Beck's work in cognitive therapy.
Cognitive distortion	Cognitive distortions are exaggerated and irrational thoughts identified in cognitive therapy and its variants, which in theory perpetuate certain psychological disorders. The theory of cognitive distortions was first proposed by David D. Burns, MD. Eliminating these distortions and negative thoughts is said to improve mood and discourage maladies such as depression and chronic anxiety. The process of learning to refute these distortions is called 'cognitive restructuring'.
Personalization	Personalization involves using technology to accommodate the differences between individuals. Once confined mainly to the Web, it is increasingly becoming a factor in education, health care (i.e. personalized medicine), television, and in both 'business to business' and 'business to consumer' settings. A good definition of personalization is the following:

Chapter 9. Cognitive-Behavioral Family Therapy

CHAPTER HIGHLIGHTS & NOTES: KEY TERMS, PEOPLE, PLACES, CONCEPTS

Selective abstraction	In clinical psychology, selective abstraction is a type of cognitive bias in which a detail is taken out of context and believed whilst everything else in the context is ignored. It commonly appears in Aaron Beck's work in cognitive therapy. Another definition is, 'focusing on only the negative aspects of an event, such as 'I ruined the whole recital because of that one mistake'.
Abstraction	Sociological Abstraction refers to the varying levels at which theoretical concepts can be understood. This idea is very similar to the philosophical understanding of abstraction. There are two basic levels of sociological abstraction: sociological concepts and operationalized sociological concepts.
Contingency management	Contingency management is a type of treatment used in the mental health or substance abuse fields. Patients' behaviors are rewarded (or, less often, punished); generally, adherence to or failure to adhere to program rules and regulations or their treatment plan. As an approach to treatment, contingency management emerged from the behavior therapy and applied behavior analysis traditions in mental health.
Shaping	The differential reinforcement of successive approximations, or more commonly, shaping is a conditioning procedure used primarily in the experimental analysis of behavior. It was introduced by B.F. Skinner with pigeons and extended to dogs, dolphins, humans and other species. In shaping, the form of an existing response is gradually changed across successive trials towards a desired target behavior by rewarding exact segments of behavior.
Token economy	A token economy is a system of behavior modification based on the systematic positive reinforcement of target behavior. The reinforcers are symbols or tokens that can be exchanged for other reinforcers. Token economy is based on the principles of operant conditioning and can be situated within applied behavior analysis (behaviorism).
Time-out	A time-out is a form of punishment that involves temporarily separating a child from an environment where inappropriate behavior has occurred, and is intended to remove positive reinforcement of the behavior. It is an educational and parenting technique recommended by some pediatricians and developmental psychologists as an effective form of child discipline. Often a corner (hence the common term corner time) or a similar space where the child is to stand or sit during time-outs is designated.
Attachment theory	Attachment theory describes the dynamics of long-term relationships between humans. Its most important tenet is that an infant needs to develop a relationship with at least one primary caregiver for social and emotional development to occur normally. Attachment theory explains how much the parents' relationship with the child influences development.
Assertiveness	Assertiveness is a particular mode of communication.

Chapter 9. Cognitive-Behavioral Family Therapy

CHAPTER HIGHLIGHTS & NOTES: KEY TERMS, PEOPLE, PLACES, CONCEPTS

	Dorland's Medical Dictionary defines assertiveness as:'a form of behavior characterized by a confident declaration or affirmation of a statement without need of proof; this affirms the person's rights or point of view without either aggressively threatening the rights of another (assuming a position of dominance) or submissively permitting another to ignore or deny one's rights or point of view.'
	During the second half of the 20th century, assertiveness was increasingly singled out as a behavioral skill taught by many personal development experts, behavior therapists, and cognitive behavioral therapists. Assertiveness is often linked to self-esteem.
Sexual dysfunction	Sexual dysfunction, including desire, arousal or orgasm.
	To maximize the benefits of medications and behavioural techniques in the management of sexual dysfunction it is important to have a comprehensive approach to the problem, A thorough sexual history and assessment of general health and other sexual problems (if any) are very important. Assessing (performance) anxiety, guilt (associated with masturbation in many Indian men), stress and worry are integral to the optimal management of sexual dysfunction.
Arousal	Arousal is a physiological and psychological state of being awake or reactive to stimuli. It involves the activation of the reticular activating system in the brain stem, the autonomic nervous system and the endocrine system, leading to increased heart rate and blood pressure and a condition of sensory alertness, mobility and readiness to respond.
	There are many different neural systems involved in what is collectively known as the arousal system.
Teasing	Teasing is a word with many meanings. In human interactions, teasing comes in two major forms, playful and hurtful. When teasing is playful and friendly, and especially when it is reciprocal, teasing can be regarded as flirting.
Parent Management Training	Parent Management Training is a programme that trains parents to manage their children's behavioural problems at home and at school. Parent Management Training works to correct maladaptive parent-child interactions especially as they apply to discipline. Parent Management Training utilizes social learning techniques based upon behaviour analysis and operant conditioning to alter both the parents' and the child's behaviour to decrease the child's oppositional or antisocial behavioural patterns.
Social learning	Social learning is learning that takes place at a wider scale than individual or group learning, up to a societal scale, through social interaction between peers. It may or may not lead to a change in attitudes and behaviour.

Chapter 9. Cognitive-Behavioral Family Therapy

CHAPTER HIGHLIGHTS & NOTES: KEY TERMS, PEOPLE, PLACES, CONCEPTS

Social learning theory	Social learning theory is derived from the work of Albert Bandura which proposed that social learning occurred through four main stages of imitation:•close contact,•imitation of superiors,•understanding of concepts,•role model behavior
	It consists of three parts: observing, imitating, and reinforcements
	Julian Rotter moved away from theories based on psychosis and behaviorism, and developed a learning theory. In Social Learning and Clinical Psychology (1945), Rotter suggests that the effect of behavior has an impact on the motivation of people to engage in that specific behavior. People wish to avoid negative consequences, while desiring positive results or effects.

CHAPTER QUIZ: KEY TERMS, PEOPLE, PLACES, CONCEPTS

1. Burrhus Frederic 'B. F.' _____ was an American psychologist, behaviorist, author, inventor, and social philosopher. He was the Edgar Pierce Professor of Psychology at Harvard University from 1958 until his retirement in 1974.

    _____ invented the operant conditioning chamber, also known as the _____ Box.

    a. Montrose Wolf
    b. B. F. Skinner
    c. Alyssa Rubino
    d. Brian McQueen

2. In psychology, _____ is defined as the diminished emotional responsiveness to a negative or aversive stimulus after repeated exposure to it. It also occurs when an emotional response is repeatedly evoked in situations in which the action tendency that is associated with the emotion proves irrelevant or unnecessary. _____ is a process primarily used to assist individuals unlearn phobias and anxieties and was developed by psychologist Mary Cover Jones.

    a. Direct therapeutic exposure
    b. Flooding
    c. Systematic desensitization
    d. Desensitization

3. . _____ is a type of behavioral therapy used in the field of psychology to help effectively overcome phobias and other anxiety disorders. More specifically, it is a type of Pavlovian therapy / classical conditioning therapy developed by a South African psychiatrist, Joseph Wolpe. To begin the process of _____, one must first be taught relaxation skills in order to extinguish fear and anxiety responses to specific phobias.

Chapter 9. Cognitive-Behavioral Family Therapy

CHAPTER QUIZ: KEY TERMS, PEOPLE, PLACES, CONCEPTS

    a. State Children's Health Insurance Program
    b. Active recall
    c. Systematic desensitization
    d. Adaptive hypermedia

4. _____ is a form of learning in which an individual's behavior is modified by its consequences; the behaviour may change in form, frequency, or strength. _____ is a term that was coined by B.F Skinner in 1937 _____ is distinguished from classical conditioning in that _____ deals with the modification of 'voluntary behaviour' or operant behaviour. Operant behavior operates on the environment and is maintained by its consequences, while classical conditioning deals with the conditioning of reflexive (reflex) behaviours which are elicited by antecedent conditions.

    a. Academic advising
    b. Active recall
    c. Operant conditioning
    d. Adaptive hypermedia

5. _____ is a word with many meanings. In human interactions, _____ comes in two major forms, playful and hurtful. When _____ is playful and friendly, and especially when it is reciprocal, _____ can be regarded as flirting.

    a. Teen dating violence
    b. Teasing
    c. Terrorism
    d. Torture

Visit Cram101.com for full Practice Exams

Visit Cram101.com for full Practice Exams

ANSWER KEY
Chapter 9. Cognitive-Behavioral Family Therapy

1. b
2. d
3. c
4. c
5. b

You can take the complete Chapter Practice Test

for Chapter 9. Cognitive-Behavioral Family Therapy
on all key terms, persons, places, and concepts.

Online 99 Cents

http://www.epub126.12.20893.9.cram101.com/

Use www.Cram101.com for all your study needs

including Cram101's online interactive problem solving labs in

chemistry, statistics, mathematics, and more.

Chapter 10. Family Therapy in the Twenty-First Century

CHAPTER OUTLINE: KEY TERMS, PEOPLE, PLACES, CONCEPTS

	Family therapy
	Narrative
	Postmodernism
	Collaborative therapy
	Constructivism
	Social constructionism
	Constructionism
	Narrative therapy
	Domestic violence
	Multiculturalism
	Social class
	Socioeconomics
	Diversity
	Amygdala
	Functional magnetic resonance imaging
	Spirituality
	Racism
	Homophobia
	Incidence

Visit Cram101.com for full Practice Exams

Chapter 10. Family Therapy in the Twenty-First Century
CHAPTER OUTLINE: KEY TERMS, PEOPLE, PLACES, CONCEPTS

_____	Case management
_____	Crisis intervention
_____	Family support
_____	Intervention
_____	Expressed emotion
_____	Psychoeducational
_____	Double bind

CHAPTER HIGHLIGHTS & NOTES: KEY TERMS, PEOPLE, PLACES, CONCEPTS

Family therapy	Family therapy, also referred to as couple and family therapy, family systems therapy, and family counseling, is a branch of psychotherapy that works with families and couples in intimate relationships to nurture change and development. It tends to view change in terms of the systems of interaction between family members. It emphasizes family relationships as an important factor in psychological health.
Narrative	A narrative is a story that is created in a constructive format (as a work of speech, writing, song, film, television, video games, photography or theatre) that describes a sequence of fictional or non-fictional events. Ultimately its origin is found in the Proto-Indo-European root gno-, 'to know'. The word 'story' may be used as a synonym of 'narrative', but can also be used to refer to the sequence of events described in a narrative.
Postmodernism	Postmodernism is a movement away from the viewpoint of modernism. More specifically it is a tendency in contemporary culture characterized by the problem of objective truth and inherent suspicion towards global cultural narrative or meta-narrative. It involves the belief that many, if not all, apparent realities are only social constructs, as they are subject to change inherent to time and place.

Visit Cram101.com for full Practice Exams

Chapter 10. Family Therapy in the Twenty-First Century

CHAPTER HIGHLIGHTS & NOTES: KEY TERMS, PEOPLE, PLACES, CONCEPTS

Collaborative therapy	'Developed by Dr. Harlene Anderson, along with Dr. Harold A. Goolishian (1924-1991), in the USA, collaborative therapy could be especially useful for those clients who are well educated in any field or for those that have distrust of therapists due to past negative experiences with one or moreCollaborative Therapy gives the client the option to have a 'non-authoritarian' counsellor. This could greatly benefit clients who are a) not heteronormative b) GID (Gender identity disorder) c) 'transgender' d) choose to live an Alternative lifestyle.'(page 1) This is because it is often they that are most subject to heteronormative evaluation, which simply is inappropriate for them and indeed can cause further harm and distress. Anderson used Collaborative Therapy in family and marriage therapy too, with great success, which could help families and partners to understand the client better should the client find that they cannot adhere to social 'norms' any more (such as 'coming out' as trans or SGR (same gender relationship)). (page 63).
Constructivism	Constructivism is a theory of learning and an approach to education that lays emphasis on the ways that people create meaning of the world through a series of individual constructs. Constructs are the different types of filters we choose to place over our realities to change our reality from chaos to order. Von Glasersfeld describes constructivism as 'a theory of knowledge with roots in philosophy, psychology, and cybernetics'.
Social constructionism	Social constructionism and social constructivism are sociological theories of knowledge that consider how social phenomena or objects of consciousness develop in social contexts. A social construction (also called a social construct) is a concept or practice that is the construct of a particular group. When we say that something is socially constructed, we are focusing on its dependence on contingent variables of our social selves rather than any inherent quality that it possesses in itself.
Constructionism	Constructionist learning is inspired by the constructivist theory that individual learners construct mental models to understand the world around them. However, constructionism holds that learning can happen most effectively when people are also active in making tangible objects in the real world. In this sense, constructionism is connected with experiential learning, and builds on Jean Piaget's epistemological theory of constructivism.
Narrative therapy	Narrative Therapy is a form of psychotherapy using narrative.

Chapter 10. Family Therapy in the Twenty-First Century

CHAPTER HIGHLIGHTS & NOTES: KEY TERMS, PEOPLE, PLACES, CONCEPTS

	It was initially developed during the 1970s and 1980s, largely by Australian Michael White and his friend and colleague, David Epston, of New Zealand.
	Their approach became prevalent in North America with the 1990 publication of their book, Narrative Means to Therapeutic Ends, followed by numerous books and articles about previously unmanageable cases of anorexia nervosa, ADHD, schizophrenia, and many other problems.
Domestic violence	Domestic violence, spousal abuse, battering, family violence, and intimate partner violence (IPV), is defined as a pattern of abusive behaviors by one partner against another in an intimate relationship such as marriage, dating, family, or cohabitation. Domestic violence, so defined, has many forms, including physical aggression or assault (hitting, kicking, biting, shoving, restraining, slapping, throwing objects), or threats thereof; sexual abuse; emotional abuse; controlling or domineering; intimidation; stalking; passive/covert abuse (e.g., neglect); and economic deprivation.
	Alcohol consumption and mental illness can be co-morbid with abuse, and present additional challenges in eliminating domestic violence.
Multiculturalism	Multiculturalism relates to communities containing multiple cultures. The term is used in two broad ways, either descriptively or normatively. As a descriptive term, it usually refers to the simple fact of cultural diversity: it is generally applied to the demographic make-up of a specific place, sometime at the organizational level, e.g. schools, businesses, neighbourhoods, cities, or nations.
Social class	Social classes are economic or cultural arrangements of groups in society. Class is an essential object of analysis for sociologists, political scientists, economists, anthropologists and social historians. In the social sciences, social class is often discussed in terms of 'social stratification'. In the modern Western context, stratification typically comprises three layers: upper class, middle class, and lower class. Each class may be further subdivided into smaller classes (e.g. occupational).
Socioeconomics	Socioeconomics is an umbrella term with different usages. 'Social economics' may refer broadly to the 'use of economics in the study of society.' More narrowly, contemporary practice considers behavioral interactions of individuals and groups through social capital and social 'markets' (not excluding for example, sorting by marriage) and the formation of social norms. In the latter, it studies the relation of economics to social values.
Diversity	In sociology and political studies, the term diversity is used to describe political entities (neighborhoods, student bodies, etc). with members who have identifiable differences in their cultural backgrounds or lifestyles.

Chapter 10. Family Therapy in the Twenty-First Century

CHAPTER HIGHLIGHTS & NOTES: KEY TERMS, PEOPLE, PLACES, CONCEPTS

Amygdala	The are almond-shaped groups of nuclei located deep within the medial temporal lobes of the brain in complex vertebrates, including humans. Shown in research to perform a primary role in the processing of memory and emotional reactions, the amygdalae are considered part of the limbic system. Anatomical subdivisions The regions described as amygdala nuclei encompass several structures with distinct connectional and functional characteristics in humans and other animals.
Functional magnetic resonance imaging	Functional magnetic resonance imaging is an MRI procedure that measures brain activity by detecting associated changes in blood flow. The primary form of fMRI uses the blood-oxygen-level-dependent (BOLD) contrast, discovered by Seiji Ogawa. This is a type of specialized brain and body scan used to map neural activity in the brain or spinal cord of humans or animals by imaging the change in blood flow (hemodynamic response) related to energy use by brain cells.
Spirituality	Spirituality is the concept of an ultimate or an alleged immaterial reality; an inner path enabling a person to discover the essence of his/her being; or the 'deepest values and meanings by which people live.' Spiritual practices, including meditation, prayer and contemplation, are intended to develop an individual's inner life. Spiritual experiences can include being connected to a larger reality, yielding a more comprehensive self; joining with other individuals or the human community; with nature or the cosmos; or with the divine realm. Spirituality is often experienced as a source of inspiration or orientation in life.
Racism	Racism is usually defined as views, practices and actions reflecting the belief that humanity is divided into distinct biological groups called races and that members of a certain race share certain attributes which make that group as a whole less desirable, more desirable, inferior or superior. The exact definition of racism is controversial both because there is little scholarly agreement about the meaning of the concept 'race', and because there is also little agreement about what does and doesn't constitute discrimination. Critics argue that the term is applied differentially, with a focus on such prejudices by whites, and defining mere observations of racial differences as racism.
Homophobia	Homophobia encompasses a range of negative attitudes and feelings toward homosexuality or people who are identified or perceived as being lesbian, gay, bisexual or transgender (LGBT). It can be expressed as antipathy, contempt, prejudice, aversion, or hatred, and may be based on irrational fear. Homophobia is observable in critical and hostile behavior such as discrimination and violence on the basis of sexual orientations that are non-heterosexual.

Chapter 10. Family Therapy in the Twenty-First Century

CHAPTER HIGHLIGHTS & NOTES: KEY TERMS, PEOPLE, PLACES, CONCEPTS

Incidence	Incidence is a measure of the risk of developing some new condition within a specified period of time. Although sometimes loosely expressed simply as the number of new cases during some time period, it is better expressed as a proportion or a rate with a denominator. Incidence proportion (also known as cumulative incidence) is the number of new cases within a specified time period divided by the size of the population initially at risk.
Case management	Case management is the coordination of community services for mental health patients by allocating a professional to be responsible for the assessment of need and implementation of care plans. It is usually required for individuals who have a serious mental illness and need ongoing support in areas such as housing, employment, social relationships, and community participation. This level of support is also suitable for service users with a major psychotic disorder.
Crisis intervention	Crisis Intervention can be defined as emergency psychological care aimed at assisting individuals in a crisis situation to restore equilibrium to their biopsychosocial functioning and to minimise the potential for psychological trauma. Crisis can be defined as one's perception or experiencing of an event or situation as an intolerable difficulty that exceeds the person's current resources and coping mechanisms. The priority of crisis intervention/counseling is to increase stabilization.
Family support	Family support is a term that has three primary uses. The first use is the general understanding that family life is best 'supported' by good relationships among family members, with extended family, neighbors, friends, and others in one's own family network. The second term began in the field of intellectual disabilities (can be found in other disability fields)and refers to an array of services, including the original parent-based service of respite and cash subsidies; secondarily, the term refers to a combination of informal support and formal services.
Intervention	An intervention is an orchestrated attempt by one or many, people - usually family and friends - to get someone to seek professional help with an addiction or some kind of traumatic event or crisis, or other serious problem. The term intervention is most often used when the traumatic event involves addiction to drugs or other items. Intervention can also refer to the act of using a similar technique within a therapy session.
Expressed emotion	Expressed emotion is a qualitative measure of the 'amount' of emotion displayed, typically in the family setting, usually by a family or care takers. Theoretically, a high level of Expressed emotion in the home can worsen the prognosis in patients with mental illness, (Brown et al., 1962, 1972) or act as a potential risk factor for the development of psychiatric disease. Typically it is determined whether a person or family has high expressed emotion or low expressed emotion through a taped interview known as the Camberwell Family Interview (CFI).

Chapter 10. Family Therapy in the Twenty-First Century

CHAPTER HIGHLIGHTS & NOTES: KEY TERMS, PEOPLE, PLACES, CONCEPTS

Double bind	A double bind is an emotionally distressing dilemma in communication in which an individual receives two or more conflicting messages, in which one message negates the other. This creates a situation in which a successful response to one message results in a failed response to the other (and vice versa), so that the person will be automatically wrong regardless of response. The double bind occurs when the person cannot confront the inherent dilemma, and therefore cannot resolve it or opt out of the situation.

CHAPTER QUIZ: KEY TERMS, PEOPLE, PLACES, CONCEPTS

1. A _____ is a story that is created in a constructive format (as a work of speech, writing, song, film, television, video games, photography or theatre) that describes a sequence of fictional or non-fictional events. Ultimately its origin is found in the Proto-Indo-European root gno-, 'to know'.

    The word 'story' may be used as a synonym of '_____', but can also be used to refer to the sequence of events described in a _____.

    a. State Children's Health Insurance Program
    b. Justice Resource Institute
    c. Narrative
    d. Mental status examination

2. _____, also referred to as couple and _____, family systems therapy, and family counseling, is a branch of psychotherapy that works with families and couples in intimate relationships to nurture change and development. It tends to view change in terms of the systems of interaction between family members. It emphasizes family relationships as an important factor in psychological health.

    a. Family therapy
    b. Justice Resource Institute
    c. Mental health professional
    d. Mental status examination

3. . _____ is a movement away from the viewpoint of modernism. More specifically it is a tendency in contemporary culture characterized by the problem of objective truth and inherent suspicion towards global cultural narrative or meta-narrative. It involves the belief that many, if not all, apparent realities are only social constructs, as they are subject to change inherent to time and place.

    a. State Children's Health Insurance Program
    b. Justice Resource Institute

Visit Cram101.com for full Practice Exams

Chapter 10. Family Therapy in the Twenty-First Century

CHAPTER QUIZ: KEY TERMS, PEOPLE, PLACES, CONCEPTS

   c. Postmodernism
   d. Mental status examination

4. Constructionist learning is inspired by the constructivist theory that individual learners construct mental models to understand the world around them. However, _____ holds that learning can happen most effectively when people are also active in making tangible objects in the real world. In this sense, _____ is connected with experiential learning, and builds on Jean Piaget's epistemological theory of constructivism.

   a. Constructionism
   b. Constructivism
   c. Cooperative learning
   d. Correspondent inference theory

5. 'Developed by Dr. Harlene Anderson, along with Dr. Harold A. Goolishian (1924-1991), in the USA, _____ could be especially useful for those clients who are well educated in any field or for those that have distrust of therapists due to past negative experiences with one or more_____ gives the client the option to have a 'non-authoritarian' counsellor. This could greatly benefit clients who are

   a) not heteronormative

   b) GID (Gender identity disorder)

   c) 'transgender'

   d) choose to live an Alternative lifestyle.'(page 1)

   This is because it is often they that are most subject to heteronormative evaluation, which simply is inappropriate for them and indeed can cause further harm and distress. Anderson used _____ in family and marriage therapy too, with great success, which could help families and partners to understand the client better should the client find that they cannot adhere to social 'norms' any more (such as 'coming out' as trans or SGR (same gender relationship)). (page 63).

   a. Continuous passive motion
   b. Dark therapy
   c. Diversional therapy
   d. Collaborative therapy

Visit Cram101.com for full Practice Exams

Visit Cram101.com for full Practice Exams

ANSWER KEY
Chapter 10. Family Therapy in the Twenty-First Century

1. c
2. a
3. c
4. a
5. d

You can take the complete Chapter Practice Test

for Chapter 10. Family Therapy in the Twenty-First Century

on all key terms, persons, places, and concepts.

Online 99 Cents

http://www.epub126.12.20893.10.cram101.com/

Use www.Cram101.com for all your study needs

including Cram101's online interactive problem solving labs in

chemistry, statistics, mathematics, and more.

Chapter 11. Solution-Focused Therapy

CHAPTER OUTLINE: KEY TERMS, PEOPLE, PLACES, CONCEPTS

- _____ Family therapy
- _____ Milton H. Erickson
- _____ Goal setting
- _____ Miracle
- _____ Exploring
- _____ Coping
- _____ Feedback

CHAPTER HIGHLIGHTS & NOTES: KEY TERMS, PEOPLE, PLACES, CONCEPTS

Family therapy	Family therapy, also referred to as couple and family therapy, family systems therapy, and family counseling, is a branch of psychotherapy that works with families and couples in intimate relationships to nurture change and development. It tends to view change in terms of the systems of interaction between family members. It emphasizes family relationships as an important factor in psychological health.
Milton H. Erickson	Milton H. Erickson, (5 December 1901 in Aurum, Nevada - 25 March 1980 in Phoenix, Arizona) was an American psychiatrist specializing in medical hypnosis and family therapy. He was founding president of the American Society for Clinical Hypnosis and a fellow of the American Psychiatric Association, the American Psychological Association, and the American Psychopathological Association. He is noted for his approach to the unconscious mind as creative and solution-generating.
Goal setting	Goal setting involves establishing specific, measurable, achievable, realistic and time-targeted (S.M.A.R.T) goals. Work on the theory of goal-setting suggests that it's an effective tool for making progress by ensuring that participants in a group with a common goal are clearly aware of what is expected from them. On a personal level, setting goals helps people work towards their own objectives-most commonly with financial or career-based goals.

Chapter 11. Solution-Focused Therapy

CHAPTER HIGHLIGHTS & NOTES: KEY TERMS, PEOPLE, PLACES, CONCEPTS

Miracle	A miracle is an event attributed to divine intervention. Alternatively, it may be an event attributed to a miracle worker, saint, or religious leader. A miracle is sometimes thought of as a perceptible interruption of the laws of nature.
Exploring	Exploring is a worksite-based program of Learning for Life, a subsidiary of the Boy Scouts of America, for young men and women who are 14 through 20 years old (15 through 21 in some areas). Exploring units, called 'posts', usually have a focus on a single career field, such as police, fire/rescue, health, law, aviation, engineering, or the like, and may be sponsored by a government or business entity. Prior to the late 1990s, the Exploring program was the main BSA program for older youth and included posts with an emphasis on outdoor activities, which are now part of the Venturing program.
Coping	Coping has been defined in psychological terms by Susan Folkman and Richard Lazarus as 'constantly changing cognitive and behavioral efforts to manage specific external and/or internal demands that are appraised as taxing' or 'exceeding the resources of the person'. Coping is thus expending conscious effort to solve personal and interpersonal problems, and seeking to master, minimize or tolerate stress or conflict. Psychological coping mechanisms are commonly termed coping strategies or coping skills.
Feedback	Feedback is a process in which information about the past or the present influences the same phenomenon in the present or future. As part of a chain of cause-and-effect that forms a circuit or loop, the event is said to 'feed back' into itself. Ramaprasad (1983) defines feedback generally as 'information about the gap between the actual level and the reference level of a system parameter which is used to alter the gap in some way', emphasising that the information by itself is not feedback unless translated into action.

Chapter 11. Solution-Focused Therapy

CHAPTER QUIZ: KEY TERMS, PEOPLE, PLACES, CONCEPTS

1. _____, also referred to as couple and _____, family systems therapy, and family counseling, is a branch of psychotherapy that works with families and couples in intimate relationships to nurture change and development. It tends to view change in terms of the systems of interaction between family members. It emphasizes family relationships as an important factor in psychological health.

    a. Gestalt therapy
    b. Justice Resource Institute
    c. Mental health professional
    d. Family therapy

2. _____, (5 December 1901 in Aurum, Nevada - 25 March 1980 in Phoenix, Arizona) was an American psychiatrist specializing in medical hypnosis and family therapy. He was founding president of the American Society for Clinical Hypnosis and a fellow of the American Psychiatric Association, the American Psychological Association, and the American Psychopathological Association. He is noted for his approach to the unconscious mind as creative and solution-generating.

    a. George Estabrooks
    b. Glenn Harrold
    c. Ernest Hilgard
    d. Milton H. Erickson

3. _____ involves establishing specific, measurable, achievable, realistic and time-targeted (S.M.A.R.T) goals. Work on the theory of goal-setting suggests that it's an effective tool for making progress by ensuring that participants in a group with a common goal are clearly aware of what is expected from them. On a personal level, setting goals helps people work towards their own objectives-most commonly with financial or career-based goals.

    a. Goal setting
    b. Glenn Harrold
    c. Ernest Hilgard
    d. Clark L. Hull

4. _____ is a process in which information about the past or the present influences the same phenomenon in the present or future. As part of a chain of cause-and-effect that forms a circuit or loop, the event is said to 'feed back' into itself.

    Ramaprasad (1983) defines _____ generally as 'information about the gap between the actual level and the reference level of a system parameter which is used to alter the gap in some way', emphasising that the information by itself is not _____ unless translated into action.

    a. State Children's Health Insurance Program
    b. Defense physiology
    c. Feedback
    d. Historical trauma

Chapter 11. Solution-Focused Therapy

CHAPTER QUIZ: KEY TERMS, PEOPLE, PLACES, CONCEPTS

5. _____ has been defined in psychological terms by Susan Folkman and Richard Lazarus as 'constantly changing cognitive and behavioral efforts to manage specific external and/or internal demands that are appraised as taxing' or 'exceeding the resources of the person'.

   _____ is thus expending conscious effort to solve personal and interpersonal problems, and seeking to master, minimize or tolerate stress or conflict. Psychological _____ mechanisms are commonly termed _____ strategies or _____ skills.

   a. Cortisol awakening response
   b. Defense physiology
   c. Freezing behavior
   d. Coping

Visit Cram101.com for full Practice Exams

ANSWER KEY
Chapter 11. Solution-Focused Therapy

1. d
2. d
3. a
4. c
5. d

You can take the complete Chapter Practice Test

for Chapter 11. Solution-Focused Therapy
on all key terms, persons, places, and concepts.

Online 99 Cents

http://www.epub126.12.20893.11.cram101.com/

Use www.Cram101.com for all your study needs

including Cram101's online interactive problem solving labs in

chemistry, statistics, mathematics, and more.

Chapter 12. Narrative Therapy

CHAPTER OUTLINE: KEY TERMS, PEOPLE, PLACES, CONCEPTS

	Narrative
	Narrative therapy
	Reframing
	Birthing center
	Michael White
	Externalization
	Anorexia nervosa
	Collaborative therapy

CHAPTER HIGHLIGHTS & NOTES: KEY TERMS, PEOPLE, PLACES, CONCEPTS

Narrative	A narrative is a story that is created in a constructive format (as a work of speech, writing, song, film, television, video games, photography or theatre) that describes a sequence of fictional or non-fictional events. Ultimately its origin is found in the Proto-Indo-European root gno-, 'to know'. The word 'story' may be used as a synonym of 'narrative', but can also be used to refer to the sequence of events described in a narrative.
Narrative therapy	Narrative Therapy is a form of psychotherapy using narrative. It was initially developed during the 1970s and 1980s, largely by Australian Michael White and his friend and colleague, David Epston, of New Zealand. Their approach became prevalent in North America with the 1990 publication of their book, Narrative Means to Therapeutic Ends, followed by numerous books and articles about previously unmanageable cases of anorexia nervosa, ADHD, schizophrenia, and many other problems.
Reframing	The term reframing designates a communication technique which has origins in family systems therapy and the work of Virginia Satir. Milton H.

Chapter 12. Narrative Therapy

CHAPTER HIGHLIGHTS & NOTES: KEY TERMS, PEOPLE, PLACES, CONCEPTS

	Erickson has been associated with reframing and it also forms an important part of Neuro-linguistic programming. In addition, provocative therapy uses reframing with an emphasis on humor.
Birthing center	A birthing center is a healthcare facility, staffed by nurse-midwives, midwives and/or obstetricians, for mothers in labor, who may be assisted by doulas and coaches. By attending the laboring mother, the doulas can assist the midwives and make the birth easier. The midwives monitor the labor, and well-being of the mother and fetus during birth.
Michael White	Michael White was an Australian social worker and family therapist.
Externalization	Externalization means to put something outside of its original borders, especially to put a human function outside of the human body. The opposite of externalization is internalization. In a concrete sense, by taking notes, we can externalize the function of memory which normally belongs in the brain.
Anorexia nervosa	The differential diagnoses of anorexia nervosa includes various types of medical and psychological conditions, which may be misdiagnosed as AN. In some cases, these conditions may be comorbid with AN because the misdiagnosis of AN is not uncommon. For example, a case of achalasia was misdiagnosed as AN and the patient spent two months confined to a psychiatric hospital. A reason for the differential diagnoses that surround AN arise mainly because, like other disorders, it is primarily, albeit defensively and adaptive for, the individual concerned.
Collaborative therapy	'Developed by Dr. Harlene Anderson, along with Dr. Harold A. Goolishian (1924-1991), in the USA, collaborative therapy could be especially useful for those clients who are well educated in any field or for those that have distrust of therapists due to past negative experiences with one or moreCollaborative Therapy gives the client the option to have a 'non-authoritarian' counsellor. This could greatly benefit clients who are a) not heteronormative b) GID (Gender identity disorder) c) 'transgender' d) choose to live an Alternative lifestyle.'(page 1) This is because it is often they that are most subject to heteronormative evaluation, which simply is inappropriate for them and indeed can cause further harm and distress.

Chapter 12. Narrative Therapy

CHAPTER QUIZ: KEY TERMS, PEOPLE, PLACES, CONCEPTS

1. _____ is a form of psychotherapy using narrative. It was initially developed during the 1970s and 1980s, largely by Australian Michael White and his friend and colleague, David Epston, of New Zealand.

   Their approach became prevalent in North America with the 1990 publication of their book, Narrative Means to Therapeutic Ends, followed by numerous books and articles about previously unmanageable cases of anorexia nervosa, ADHD, schizophrenia, and many other problems.

   a. Narrative therapy
   b. Neuropsychological test
   c. Paced Auditory Serial Addition Test
   d. Person-centered therapy

2. A _____ is a story that is created in a constructive format (as a work of speech, writing, song, film, television, video games, photography or theatre) that describes a sequence of fictional or non-fictional events. Ultimately its origin is found in the Proto-Indo-European root gno-, 'to know'.

   The word 'story' may be used as a synonym of '_____', but can also be used to refer to the sequence of events described in a _____.

   a. Narrative
   b. The Kallikak Family
   c. Bretton Woods system
   d. The Children of Sanchez

3. . 'Developed by Dr. Harlene Anderson, along with Dr. Harold A. Goolishian (1924-1991), in the USA, _____ could be especially useful for those clients who are well educated in any field or for those that have distrust of therapists due to past negative experiences with one or more_____ gives the client the option to have a 'non-authoritarian' counsellor. This could greatly benefit clients who are

   a) not heteronormative

   b) GID (Gender identity disorder)

   c) 'transgender'

   d) choose to live an Alternative lifestyle.'(page 1)

   This is because it is often they that are most subject to heteronormative evaluation, which simply is inappropriate for them and indeed can cause further harm and distress. Anderson used _____ in family and marriage therapy too, with great success, which could help families and partners to understand the client better should the client find that they cannot adhere to social 'norms' any more (such as 'coming out' as trans or SGR (same gender relationship)). (page 63).

   a. Continuous passive motion

Visit Cram101.com for full Practice Exams

Chapter 12. Narrative Therapy

CHAPTER QUIZ: KEY TERMS, PEOPLE, PLACES, CONCEPTS

    b. Dark therapy
    c. Diversional therapy
    d. Collaborative therapy

4. _____ was an Australian social worker and family therapist.

    a. Diane Youdale
    b. Michael White
    c. Eberhard Schorsch
    d. Emmy van Deurzen

5. The term _____ designates a communication technique which has origins in family systems therapy and the work of Virginia Satir. Milton H. Erickson has been associated with _____ and it also forms an important part of Neuro-linguistic programming. In addition, provocative therapy uses _____ with an emphasis on humor.

    a. Reframing
    b. Residential treatment center
    c. Response-based therapy
    d. Retman

Visit Cram101.com for full Practice Exams

ANSWER KEY
Chapter 12. Narrative Therapy

1. a
2. a
3. d
4. b
5. a

You can take the complete Chapter Practice Test

for Chapter 12. Narrative Therapy
on all key terms, persons, places, and concepts.

Online 99 Cents

http://www.epub126.12.20893.12.cram101.com/

Use www.Cram101.com for all your study needs

including Cram101's online interactive problem solving labs in

chemistry, statistics, mathematics, and more.

Visit Cram101.com for full Practice Exams

Chapter 13. Comparative Analysis

99

CHAPTER OUTLINE: KEY TERMS, PEOPLE, PLACES, CONCEPTS

_____ Family therapy

_____ Virginia Satir

_____ Triangulation

_____ Agoraphobia

_____ Differentiation

_____ Individuation

_____ Transference

_____ Scapegoating

_____ Social exchange theory

_____ Dysfunctional family

_____ Michael White

_____ Double bind

_____ Externalization

_____ Narrative

_____ Dialectical behavior therapy

_____ Mindfulness

_____ Social learning

_____ Social learning theory

Visit Cram101.com for full Practice Exams

Chapter 13. Comparative Analysis

CHAPTER HIGHLIGHTS & NOTES: KEY TERMS, PEOPLE, PLACES, CONCEPTS

Family therapy	Family therapy, also referred to as couple and family therapy, family systems therapy, and family counseling, is a branch of psychotherapy that works with families and couples in intimate relationships to nurture change and development. It tends to view change in terms of the systems of interaction between family members. It emphasizes family relationships as an important factor in psychological health.
Virginia Satir	Virginia Satir was an American author and psychotherapist, known especially for her approach to family therapy and her work with Systemic Constellations. She is widely regarded as the 'Mother of Family Therapy' Her most well-known books are Conjoint Family Therapy, 1964, Peoplemaking, 1972, and The New Peoplemaking, 1988. She is also known for creating the Virginia Satir Change Process Model, a psychological model developed through clinical studies.
Triangulation	Triangulation is most commonly used to express a situation in which one family member will not communicate directly with another family member, but will communicate with a third family member, which can lead to the third family member becoming part of the triangle. The concept originated in the study of dysfunctional family systems, but can describe behaviors in other systems as well, including work. Triangulation can also be used as a label for a form of 'splitting' in which one person plays the third family member against one that he or she is upset about.
Agoraphobia	Agoraphobia is an anxiety disorder characterized by anxiety in situations where the sufferer perceives the environment as being difficult to escape or get help. These situations include, but are not limited to, wide-open spaces, as well as uncontrollable social situations such as may be met in shopping malls, airports, and on bridges. Agoraphobia is defined within the DSM-IV TR as a subset of panic disorder, involving the fear of incurring a panic attack in those environments.
Differentiation	Differentiation is a term in system theory (found in sociology). From the viewpoint of this theory, the principal feature of modern society is the increased process of system differentiation as a way of dealing with the complexity of its environment. This is accomplished through the creation of subsystems in an effort to copy within a system the difference between it and the environment.
Individuation	The principium individuationis, or principle of individuation, describes the manner in which a thing is identified as distinguished from other things. The term is used to describe two different (though related) concepts.

Chapter 13. Comparative Analysis

CHAPTER HIGHLIGHTS & NOTES: KEY TERMS, PEOPLE, PLACES, CONCEPTS

Transference	Transference is a phenomenon in psychoanalysis characterized by unconscious redirection of feelings from one person to another. One definition of transference is 'the inappropriate repetition in the present of a relationship that was important in a person's childhood.' Another definition is 'the redirection of feelings and desires and especially of those unconsciously retained from childhood toward a new object.' Still another definition is 'a reproduction of emotions relating to repressed experiences, esp[ecially] of childhood, and the substitution of another person ... for the original object of the repressed impulses.' Transference was first described by Sigmund Freud, who acknowledged its importance for psychoanalysis for better understanding of the patient's feelings. Occurrence It is common for people to transfer feelings from their parents to their partners or children (i.e., cross-generational entanglements).
Scapegoating	Scapegoating is the practice of singling out any party for unmerited negative treatment or blame as a scapegoat. Scapegoating may be conducted by individuals against individuals (e.g. 'Hattie Francis did it, not me!'), individuals against groups (e.g., 'I failed because our school favors boys'), groups against individuals (e.g., 'Jane was the reason our team didn't win'), and groups against groups (e.g., 'Immigrants are taking all of the jobs'). A scapegoat may be an adult, sibling, child, employee, peer, ethnic or religious group, or country.
Social exchange theory	Social exchange theory is a social psychological and sociological perspective that explains social change and stability as a process of negotiated exchanges between parties. Social exchange theory posits that all human relationships are formed by the use of a subjective cost-benefit analysis and the comparison of alternatives. The theory has roots in economics, psychology and sociology.
Dysfunctional family	A dysfunctional family is a family in which conflict, misbehavior, and often child neglect or abuse on the part of individual parents occur continually and regularly, leading other members to accommodate such actions. Children sometimes grow up in such families with the understanding that such an arrangement is normal. Dysfunctional families are primarily a result of co-dependent adults, and may also be affected by addictions, such as substance abuse (alcohol, drugs, etc)., or sometimes an untreated mental illness.
Michael White	Michael White was an Australian social worker and family therapist.
Double bind	A double bind is an emotionally distressing dilemma in communication in which an individual receives two or more conflicting messages, in which one message negates the other.

Chapter 13. Comparative Analysis

CHAPTER HIGHLIGHTS & NOTES: KEY TERMS, PEOPLE, PLACES, CONCEPTS

	This creates a situation in which a successful response to one message results in a failed response to the other (and vice versa), so that the person will be automatically wrong regardless of response. The double bind occurs when the person cannot confront the inherent dilemma, and therefore cannot resolve it or opt out of the situation.
Externalization	Externalization means to put something outside of its original borders, especially to put a human function outside of the human body. The opposite of externalization is internalization.
	In a concrete sense, by taking notes, we can externalize the function of memory which normally belongs in the brain.
Narrative	A narrative is a story that is created in a constructive format (as a work of speech, writing, song, film, television, video games, photography or theatre) that describes a sequence of fictional or non-fictional events. Ultimately its origin is found in the Proto-Indo-European root gno-, 'to know'.
	The word 'story' may be used as a synonym of 'narrative', but can also be used to refer to the sequence of events described in a narrative.
Dialectical behavior therapy	Dialectical behavior therapy is a system of therapy originally developed by Marsha M. Linehan, a psychology researcher at the University of Washington, to treat people with borderline personality disorder (BPD). Dialectical behavior therapy combines standard cognitive-behavioral techniques for emotion regulation and reality-testing with concepts of distress tolerance, acceptance, and mindful awareness largely derived from Buddhist meditative practice. Dialectical behavior therapy may be the first therapy that has been experimentally demonstrated to be generally effective in treating BPD. A meta-analysis found that Dialectical behavior therapy reached moderate effects.
Mindfulness	Modern clinical psychology and psychiatry since the 1970s have developed a number of therapeutic applications based on the concept of mindfulness in Buddhist meditation.
	Several definitions of mindfulness have been used in modern psychology. According to various prominent psychological definitions, Mindfulness refers to a psychological quality that involves'
	bringing one's complete attention to the present experience on a moment-to-moment basis,'
	or involves'
	paying attention in a particular way: on purpose, in the present moment, and nonjudgmentally,'
	or involves'

Chapter 13. Comparative Analysis

CHAPTER HIGHLIGHTS & NOTES: KEY TERMS, PEOPLE, PLACES, CONCEPTS

	a kind of nonelaborative, nonjudgmental, present-centered awareness in which each thought, feeling, or sensation that arises in the attentional field is acknowledged and accepted as it is'
	Bishop, Lau, and colleagues (2004) offered a two component model of mindfulness:'
	The first component [of mindfulness] involves the self-regulation of attention so that it is maintained on immediate experience, thereby allowing for increased recognition of mental events in the present moment.'
Social learning	Social learning is learning that takes place at a wider scale than individual or group learning, up to a societal scale, through social interaction between peers. It may or may not lead to a change in attitudes and behaviour. More specifically, to be considered social learning, a process must: (1) demonstrate that a change in understanding has taken place in the individuals involved; (2) demonstrate that this change goes beyond the individual and becomes situated within wider social units or communities of practice; and (3) occur through social interactions and processes between actors within a social network (Reed et al., 2010).
Social learning theory	Social learning theory is derived from the work of Albert Bandura which proposed that social learning occurred through four main stages of imitation:•close contact,•imitation of superiors,•understanding of concepts,•role model behavior
	It consists of three parts: observing, imitating, and reinforcements
	Julian Rotter moved away from theories based on psychosis and behaviorism, and developed a learning theory. In Social Learning and Clinical Psychology (1945), Rotter suggests that the effect of behavior has an impact on the motivation of people to engage in that specific behavior. People wish to avoid negative consequences, while desiring positive results or effects.

Chapter 13. Comparative Analysis

CHAPTER QUIZ: KEY TERMS, PEOPLE, PLACES, CONCEPTS

1. _____ is a term in system theory (found in sociology). From the viewpoint of this theory, the principal feature of modern society is the increased process of system _____ as a way of dealing with the complexity of its environment. This is accomplished through the creation of subsystems in an effort to copy within a system the difference between it and the environment.

    a. Dominant culture
    b. Differentiation
    c. Dyad
    d. Dynamic density

2. _____, also referred to as couple and _____, family systems therapy, and family counseling, is a branch of psychotherapy that works with families and couples in intimate relationships to nurture change and development. It tends to view change in terms of the systems of interaction between family members. It emphasizes family relationships as an important factor in psychological health.

    a. Gestalt therapy
    b. Justice Resource Institute
    c. Family therapy
    d. Mental status examination

3. _____ was an American author and psychotherapist, known especially for her approach to family therapy and her work with Systemic Constellations. She is widely regarded as the 'Mother of Family Therapy' Her most well-known books are Conjoint Family Therapy, 1964, Peoplemaking, 1972, and The New Peoplemaking, 1988.

    She is also known for creating the _____ Change Process Model, a psychological model developed through clinical studies.

    a. Helga Schachinger
    b. Kirk J. Schneider
    c. Virginia Satir
    d. Gary Schwartz

4. . _____ is most commonly used to express a situation in which one family member will not communicate directly with another family member, but will communicate with a third family member, which can lead to the third family member becoming part of the triangle. The concept originated in the study of dysfunctional family systems, but can describe behaviors in other systems as well, including work.

    _____ can also be used as a label for a form of 'splitting' in which one person plays the third family member against one that he or she is upset about.

    a. State Children's Health Insurance Program
    b. Kirk J. Schneider
    c. Erich Schrger

Visit Cram101.com for full Practice Exams

Chapter 13. Comparative Analysis

CHAPTER QUIZ: KEY TERMS, PEOPLE, PLACES, CONCEPTS

5. _____ is a phenomenon in psychoanalysis characterized by unconscious redirection of feelings from one person to another. One definition of _____ is 'the inappropriate repetition in the present of a relationship that was important in a person's childhood.' Another definition is 'the redirection of feelings and desires and especially of those unconsciously retained from childhood toward a new object.' Still another definition is 'a reproduction of emotions relating to repressed experiences, esp[ecially] of childhood, and the substitution of another person ... for the original object of the repressed impulses.' _____ was first described by Sigmund Freud, who acknowledged its importance for psychoanalysis for better understanding of the patient's feelings.

Occurrence

It is common for people to transfer feelings from their parents to their partners or children (i.e., cross-generational entanglements).

a. True self and false self
b. Wish fulfillment
c. Transference
d. British Psychoanalytic Council

Visit Cram101.com for full Practice Exams

Visit Cram101.com for full Practice Exams

ANSWER KEY
Chapter 13. Comparative Analysis

1. b
2. c
3. c
4. d
5. c

You can take the complete Chapter Practice Test

for Chapter 13. Comparative Analysis
on all key terms, persons, places, and concepts.

Online 99 Cents

http://www.epub126.12.20893.13.cram101.com/

Use www.Cram101.com for all your study needs

including Cram101's online interactive problem solving labs in

chemistry, statistics, mathematics, and more.

Chapter 14. Research on Family Intervention

CHAPTER OUTLINE: KEY TERMS, PEOPLE, PLACES, CONCEPTS

- _____ Evidence-based practice
- _____ Program evaluation
- _____ Sleeper effect
- _____ Conduct disorder
- _____ Mediation
- _____ Childhood
- _____ Intervention
- _____ Substance abuse
- _____ Anxiety
- _____ Depression
- _____ Attachment disorder
- _____ Expressed emotion
- _____ Psychoeducational
- _____ Family therapy

Visit Cram101.com for full Practice Exams

Chapter 14. Research on Family Intervention

CHAPTER HIGHLIGHTS & NOTES: KEY TERMS, PEOPLE, PLACES, CONCEPTS

Evidence-based practice	The term evidence-based practice or empirically-supported treatment (EST) refers to preferential use of mental and behavioral health interventions for which systematic empirical research has provided evidence of statistically significant effectiveness as treatments for specific problems. In recent years, Evidence based practice has been stressed by professional organizations such as the American Psychological Association, the American Occupational Therapy Association, the American Nurses Association, and the American Physical Therapy Association, which have also strongly recommended their members to carry out investigations to provide evidence supporting or rejecting the use of specific interventions. Equivalent recommendations apply to the Canadian equivalent of these associations.
Program evaluation	Program evaluation is a systematic method for collecting, analyzing, and using information to answer questions about projects, policies and programs, particularly about their effectiveness and efficiency. In both the public and private sectors, stakeholders will want to know if the programs they are funding, implementing, voting for, receiving or objecting to are actually having the intended effect (and to what cost). This definition focuses on the question of whether the program, policy or project has, as indicated, the intended effect.
Sleeper effect	The sleeper effect is a psychological phenomenon whereby a highly persuasive message, paired with a discounting cue, causes an individual to be more persuaded by the message (rather than less persuaded) over time. The sleeper effect

When people are normally exposed to a highly persuasive message (such as an engaging or persuasive television ad), their attitudes toward the advocacy of the message display a significant increase.

Over time, however, their newly formed attitudes seem to gravitate back toward the position held prior to receiving the message, almost as if they were never exposed to the communication in the first place. |
| Conduct disorder | Conduct disorder is a psychological disorder diagnosed in childhood that presents itself through a repetitive and persistent pattern of behavior in which the basic rights of others or major age-appropriate norms are violated. These behaviors are 'antisocial behaviors.' Indeed, the disorder is often seen as the precursor to antisocial personality disorder. Diagnosis

Conduct disorder is classified in the DSM. It is diagnosed based on a prolonged pattern of antisocial behaviour such as serious violation of laws and social norms and rules. |
| Mediation | Mediation, as used in law, is a form of alternative dispute resolution (ADR), a way of resolving disputes between two or more parties with concrete effects. Typically, a third party, the mediator, assists the parties to negotiate a settlement. |

Chapter 14. Research on Family Intervention

CHAPTER HIGHLIGHTS & NOTES: KEY TERMS, PEOPLE, PLACES, CONCEPTS

Childhood	Childhood is the age span ranging from birth to adolescence. In developmental psychology, childhood is divided up into the developmental stages of toddlerhood (learning to walk), early childhood middle childhood and adolescence (puberty through post-puberty). Age ranges of childhood The term childhood is non-specific and can imply a varying range of years in human development.
Intervention	An intervention is an orchestrated attempt by one or many, people - usually family and friends - to get someone to seek professional help with an addiction or some kind of traumatic event or crisis, or other serious problem. The term intervention is most often used when the traumatic event involves addiction to drugs or other items. Intervention can also refer to the act of using a similar technique within a therapy session.
Substance abuse	Substance abuse, is a patterned use of a substance (drug) in which the user consumes the substance in amounts or with methods neither approved nor supervised by medical professionals. Substance abuse/drug abuse is not limited to mood-altering or psycho-active drugs. If an activity is performed using the objects against the rules and policies of the matter (as in steroids for performance enhancement in sports), it is also called substance abuse.
Anxiety	Anxiety is a psychological and physiological state characterized by somatic, emotional, cognitive, and behavioral components. It is the displeasing feeling of fear and concern. The root meaning of the word anxiety is 'to vex or trouble'; in either presence or absence of psychological stress, anxiety can create feelings of fear, worry, uneasiness, and dread.
Depression	Depression is a state of low mood and aversion to activity that can affect a person's thoughts, behavior, feelings and physical well-being. Depressed people may feel sad, anxious, empty, hopeless, helpless, worthless, guilty, irritable, or restless. They may lose interest in activities that once were pleasurable; experience loss of appetite or overeating, have problems concentrating, remembering details, or making decisions; and may contemplate or attempt suicide.
Attachment disorder	Attachment disorder is a broad term intended to describe disorders of mood, behavior, and social relationships arising from a failure to form normal attachments to primary care giving figures in early childhood, resulting in problematic social expectations and behaviors. Such a failure would result from unusual early experiences of neglect, abuse, abrupt separation from caregivers after about 6 months of age but before about three years of age, frequent change of caregivers or excessive numbers of caregivers, or lack of caregiver responsiveness to child communicative efforts. A problematic history of social relationships occurring after about age three may be distressing to a child, but does not result in attachment disorder.

Chapter 14. Research on Family Intervention

CHAPTER HIGHLIGHTS & NOTES: KEY TERMS, PEOPLE, PLACES, CONCEPTS

Expressed emotion	Expressed emotion is a qualitative measure of the 'amount' of emotion displayed, typically in the family setting, usually by a family or care takers. Theoretically, a high level of Expressed emotion in the home can worsen the prognosis in patients with mental illness, (Brown et al., 1962, 1972) or act as a potential risk factor for the development of psychiatric disease. Typically it is determined whether a person or family has high expressed emotion or low expressed emotion through a taped interview known as the Camberwell Family Interview (CFI).
Psychoeducational	Psychoeducational assessment and intervention target a student's function within his or her educational setting.
Family therapy	Family therapy, also referred to as couple and family therapy, family systems therapy, and family counseling, is a branch of psychotherapy that works with families and couples in intimate relationships to nurture change and development. It tends to view change in terms of the systems of interaction between family members. It emphasizes family relationships as an important factor in psychological health.

CHAPTER QUIZ: KEY TERMS, PEOPLE, PLACES, CONCEPTS

1. An _____ is an orchestrated attempt by one or many, people - usually family and friends - to get someone to seek professional help with an addiction or some kind of traumatic event or crisis, or other serious problem. The term _____ is most often used when the traumatic event involves addiction to drugs or other items. _____ can also refer to the act of using a similar technique within a therapy session.

    a. Online counseling
    b. Intervention
    c. United to End Racism
    d. Birth in Sri Lanka

2. . _____ is a systematic method for collecting, analyzing, and using information to answer questions about projects, policies and programs, particularly about their effectiveness and efficiency. In both the public and private sectors, stakeholders will want to know if the programs they are funding, implementing, voting for, receiving or objecting to are actually having the intended effect (and to what cost). This definition focuses on the question of whether the program, policy or project has, as indicated, the intended effect.

    a. Program process monitoring
    b. Proof of concept
    c. Program evaluation

Chapter 14. Research on Family Intervention

CHAPTER QUIZ: KEY TERMS, PEOPLE, PLACES, CONCEPTS

3. _____, as used in law, is a form of alternative dispute resolution (ADR), a way of resolving disputes between two or more parties with concrete effects. Typically, a third party, the mediator, assists the parties to negotiate a settlement. Disputants may mediate disputes in a variety of domains, such as commercial, legal, diplomatic, workplace, community and family matters.

    a. Memorandum of agreement
    b. Muslim Arbitration Tribunal
    c. Mediation
    d. Negotiated order

4. _____, also referred to as couple and _____, family systems therapy, and family counseling, is a branch of psychotherapy that works with families and couples in intimate relationships to nurture change and development. It tends to view change in terms of the systems of interaction between family members. It emphasizes family relationships as an important factor in psychological health.

    a. Gestalt therapy
    b. Justice Resource Institute
    c. Family therapy
    d. Mental status examination

5. The _____ is a psychological phenomenon whereby a highly persuasive message, paired with a discounting cue, causes an individual to be more persuaded by the message (rather than less persuaded) over time. The _____

    When people are normally exposed to a highly persuasive message (such as an engaging or persuasive television ad), their attitudes toward the advocacy of the message display a significant increase.

    Over time, however, their newly formed attitudes seem to gravitate back toward the position held prior to receiving the message, almost as if they were never exposed to the communication in the first place.

    a. Social cognition
    b. Sleeper effect
    c. Spatial relation
    d. Spatial-temporal reasoning

Visit Cram101.com for full Practice Exams

ANSWER KEY
Chapter 14. Research on Family Intervention

1. b
2. c
3. c
4. c
5. b

You can take the complete Chapter Practice Test

for Chapter 14. Research on Family Intervention
on all key terms, persons, places, and concepts.

Online 99 Cents

http://www.epub126.12.20893.14.cram101.com/

Use www.Cram101.com for all your study needs

including Cram101's online interactive problem solving labs in

chemistry, statistics, mathematics, and more.

Other Cram101 e-Books and Tests

Want More?
Cram101.com...

Cram101.com provides the outlines and highlights of your textbooks, just like this e-StudyGuide, but also gives you the PRACTICE TESTS, and other exclusive study tools for all of your textbooks.

Learn More. *Just click*
http://www.cram101.com/

Visit Cram101.com for full Practice Exams

Visit Cram101.com for full Practice Exams

CPSIA information can be obtained at www.ICGtesting.com
nted in the USA
W05s0511250913

4BV00001B/51/P

9 781478 461975